A Sense of Place:
My Life and Times on Roaring Creek

Chris R. Hughes

BookLocker

Saint Petersburg, Florida

Print ISBN: 978-1-64719-681-3
Ebook ISBN: 978-1-64719-682-0

Published by BookLocker.com, Inc., St. Petersburg, Florida.

Printed on acid-free paper.

Library of Congress Cataloguing in Publication Data
Hughes, Chris R.
A Sense of Place: My Life and Times on Roaring Creek by Chris R. Hughes
Library of Congress Control Number: 2021912279

BookLocker.com, Inc.
2021

First Edition

Dedicatory

Dedicated to the memory of my salt-of-the-earth parents, George and Pauline Hughes; my paternal grandparents, Robert and Nellie King Hughes; my maternal grandparents, Jack and Hazel Oaks Hughes; my Great Grandfather, Rev. James Garfield Hughes; and my sister, Pamela Hughes Elder.

Acknowledgements

My amazing wife, Tonia, is my biggest fan, my very best critic, the best person I know, and the only one I know who could abide my many idiosyncrasies for nearly forty years.

On a blustery early-March evening, the entrance into the world of my precious daughter, Amber ("a jewel," and definitely my little jewel), forever altered both the course and the demeanor of my life in a very positive manner.

I am indebted to every teacher, professor, and friend who encouraged me in the painstaking but gratifying development of the art and science of writing.

I also wish to acknowledge all of the incredibly supportive family and friends who have gently pushed and loudly encouraged me to complete this project that took way longer than intended. The completion of this book was nothing short of a compelling obligation. I can now check this project off my bucket list, if for no one else, at least for them.

Contents

Chapter 1: There's No Home Like Place

Nearly fourteen Autumns ago, on a frigid, mid-November Saturday, I watched a solitary beech leaf gracefully pirouette to the forest floor. Waving goodbye to kinder, gentler seasons, her life-filled green had been surrendered in exchange for a brittle brown. It would be her final performance. She had fulfilled her purpose, and was now destined to join her millions of other companions—hickory, oak, maple, ash, buckeye, poplar, birch, locust, other beech. She would eventually become part of the cool black earth, where her original roots still stretched.

Winter came early to the valley that year. November was usually moderate. Normal for the eleventh month in the higher altitude Blue Ridge Mountains, meant heavy frosts, much cooler weather than that of early Fall, and maybe a flake or three of snow, but not that year. It was as if gruff, sullen Old Man Winter, with his long white beard and bushy brow crusted over with frost, his breath billowing in the cutting air, had bullied and elbowed his way into late Fall. He was unwilling to wait his turn for only six more weeks or so. The sharp air clawed at my face. The frozen ground crunched beneath my boots. Snow had already fallen, and more was waiting in the wing. Blue spirals of wood smoke, rising from the chimneys of mostly humble dwellings in the valley below, were whipped and tossed by the cold air.

Standing at around 4000 feet and facing East, I scanned the valley that lay below. Length-wise, it stretches about two miles to my left, and three to my right. At its widest, it's only about a mile or two between the steep eastern and western mountain slopes. Old, melodramatic gospel songs played on the stage of memory—*Here Today, And Gone Tomorrow; Gone Home; Precious Memories;* et al.

In that moment, in that place, it was impossible for me to absorb that scene apart from thoughts of my own mortality and the never-ending cycle of change. The majority of my people are now merely apparitions of memory, no doubt rising in the swirling smoke I saw below. Heraclitus (535 BCE – 475 BCE), one of the Greek sages of yore, surely got it right when he famously stated, "The only constant is change."

At the time, daddy had been gone nearly three years, mommy was 80, and would pass less than five years later. My oldest sister, Pam, the Avery County High homecoming queen of 1971, died much too young in 1989. Baptist preacher, Great Grandpa 'Field (Garfield), Grandpa Jack, Grandma Hazel, Grandpa Rob, Grandma Nell—gone. Uncle Michael, Veral, Coda, Grady, Autie, Lloyd, Verna, Earschel, Carm, Harriet, Clay, Opal, Homer—gone. Like a wispy fog desperately clinging to the treetops on some Blue Ridge Mountain peak, only to be swept away by the Northwest wind, all were gone. All had been borne away on the gossamer wings of death.

Scores of others from the Valley, too numerous to mention, have finished their courses since that Saturday afternoon, but the Valley remains. It was there before any of us were born, and it'll be there after we are no more than names on a headstone, mere footnotes in time, *if* we are mentioned at all. Those haunting old blue ridges and narrow valleys were ancient when the great pyramids of the Nile Valley were still new, donning their blindingly brilliant coats of gleaming white limestone.

Place is powerful for those of us who have a sense of it. Some, through no fault of their own, don't have that sense, simply because they *cannot*. Some come from military families, some have had numerous job transfers, personal crises, etc. *Place* to me is what a magnet is to iron. It's almost an irrational pull, more akin to a spell of some sort. I can't explain it. Too, I'm almost afraid that if I could explain it, the charm, the lure, the magic would disappear like a soap bubble colliding with a thorn tree.

I've watched some of those incredible nature shows in utter astonishment. Certain birds, fish, and butterflies will migrate thousands of miles from the place of their origin, only to return to that exact spot, perpetuating the life cycle of their kind. They have no GPS, no compass, no map. They have only an innate *Sense of Place.*

To the ancient Israelites, as well as some of their contemporary descendants, it was as if a *Sense of Place* were programmed into their DNA. In large part, the religion of ancient Israel was by no means a purely spiritual or religious affair. Law, ritual, and culture, in and of themselves, always seemed to be weighed in the balances and found wanting, apart from *Place.* It was imprinted on the collective consciousness of the people.

No wonder the famous singers and musicians of ancient Judah, living in exile about a thousand miles from home in the 7th Century BCE, just couldn't find a melody, just couldn't muster the will, and just couldn't play a tune on their harps and lyres if they tried. Their captors begged them, taunting them perhaps, "We hear you Jews can really sing! Sing us one of your songs!" The Jews responded with, "How can we sing the LORD's song in a strange land?" And they didn't. They hung their harps on willow trees and wept (Psalm 137). I get that. Song apart from *Place* just wasn't the same. That only would have exacerbated the pain.

I'm not well-traveled, but within my limited experience, I have seen some beautiful country. I think that Stoney Creek, in Upper East Tennessee, is a picturesque kind of place, with dozens of veiny roads and hollers connecting to the main artery, but it's not *my* creek. The Great Smokeys, close to a hundred miles southwest of the Valley, are breathtaking, impressive, intimidating, but they're not *my* mountains. Shady Valley and Siam Valley, also in Upper East Tennessee, and Shenandoah Valley in western Virginia are as pretty as any valleys I'd ever hope to see, but they're not *mine*. Holston Mountain, just a stone's throw from my current dwelling, is heartbreakingly beautiful, caressing the sky with its long elegant ridgeline, but it's not *my* mountain.

I once had the privilege of looking up at Mount Hermon, at the northernmost extreme of Israel, straddling the border between Israel, Lebanon, and Syria. Over 9000 feet in elevation, the mountain's summit was still partially covered with snow in early June. That area reminded me slightly of the Roan Highlands. Spiritually and emotionally moving as it was to be there, the Roan Highlands it is not. All the aforementioned are magnificent, yet none has ever held me with such an umbilical connection as has my *Place*.

Almost entirely, my world is a forgotten one. During my college and seminary years, I remember hearing, with reference to the two primary languages of the Biblical text—Biblical Hebrew and Koine Greek—the term "dead languages." It is very true that Biblical Hebrew and Koine Greek are indeed "dead" in terms of their no longer being spoken or written languages in modern times. But, as one of my professors astutely observed, they've *never* been dead to the world of scholarship. In that realm at least, they are very much alive and well.

My world, i.e., my original point of reference, is largely *dead* in terms of culture, lifestyle, and existential reality. For those of us, however, whose moorings are tied to *Place*, it will *never* be just another fossilized relic of a past epoch. Its ghosts will haunt our memories. Its melodies will always find a way to be heard. Its stories will always beg to be told to eager ears.

Thin as onion skin paper, and bubbly as soap suds, the twenty-something year old hostess at the NASA Space Center's *Meet the Astronauts* program, faced the daunting challenge of pepping up the wilted crowd gathered for the show. Being one of the "wiltees" in the oppressive Florida heat and humidity that August afternoon, in the mid-1980's, I know that there weren't many enthusiastic participants. I did have to give the bubbly girl an A+ for effort though.

"*Hooow* many of you have ever wanted to be an astronaut?" she yelled into the microphone, her high-pitched voice resonating with rising emphasis, penetrating what eardrums I still had left. As expected, that got a response. Hands flew up all over the tin covered pavilion, that had been transformed into an oven, beneath the Florida sun.

For a very good reason, Miss 20-Something-Peppy-What's-Her-Name didn't see my hand raised. Not only was I not in the mood to participate in a pep rally, but I was also just being honest. I didn't raise my hand for one simple reason: *never*, not even *once* that I recall, have I *ever* had any inkling of a desire to be an astronaut. "Not even as a little boy?" you wonder. Nope. Nor did the thought cross my mind as a big boy either. Not even during that period of temporary insanity known as adolescence did I experience a hormonal impulse to be an astronaut. When I was five, I did aspire to the U.S. presidency, but had no aspirations of exploring the final frontier.

My reasons? Well, there are several, not least of which is the fact that something as innocuous as riding in the back seat of a car, used to have the potential to induce me toward projectile vomiting. I don't even want to think about the gastronomical effects of traveling at several thousand miles per hour at zero gravity. Nor would I want to endure the torturous training that astronauts have to complete.

The main reason I've never wanted to be an astronaut is because I've always had a gnawing fear that the spacecraft might not make it back. On the highway, it's one thing to run out of gas, or have a flat tire, or a broken transmission, but imagine having a breakdown on Mars. Or you're out only God knows where, on the intergalactic interstate at mile marker 6 quintillion. Who are you going to call? I'm pretty sure that AAA doesn't do service calls that far out. What if it's a problem Houston can't fix? Worse yet, what if something really got fouled up and you got lost in the coldness of space?

I'm very much aware that both public and private space programs are in the hands of people with big brains, super computers, and are supported with mega bucks. I know, it's all computerized, mechanized, and preprogrammed. It's not *likely* that there'd be a breakdown on the intergalactic super highway. Nor is it probable that something would so irreparably malfunction so as to miscalculate the path of travel, thus rendering the craft as MIA. But what if something *did* happen? I'll never take that chance. I just want to be able to walk back home if need be. I feel like my cousin Eric who said, "I don't want to go anywhere that I can't walk back home if I need to!" I've decided to subscribe to that way of thinking. After doing three of them, I don't even want to do another cruise.

In her formative years, my daughter Amber, along with my wife, Tonia, would sometimes accompany me to my folks' place on Roaring Creek. Since, thanks be to God, I have never truly "grown up," Amber and I would play for hours in the great outdoors. Whether swinging from the tire swing that hung from the big willow tree, riding our sleds in the deep winter snow, or just turning over rocks and finding crayfish and salamanders, we had a blast—just a little girl, and a big boy who happened to be her father. One day, with the spontaneous excitement that only a child could express, Amber exclaimed, "Dad! This place is better than Disney!" She had been to lots more theme parks than I, and thus had something with which to compare it. All along, I just assumed the truth of what she said.

Maybe you grew up in a similar world as mine, or perhaps mine is a world of which you've only heard. Trust me, it does exist. For better, for worse, for good, for ill—and it can be any of those separately or simultaneously—Roaring Creek Valley is where my roots run deep in the pitch-black dirt, sustained by the ice-cold spring waters. Welcome to *my* world. Walk the ridges, fields, and hollows with me. Throw some rocks in the roiling creek, drink your fill from its chilly springs, gaze deeply at its stunning natural beauty, listen closely to its melodies.

Surely, all honest, thinking people have regrets, but to have had the privilege of growing up where and when I did is something that I consider to be one of my greatest, choicest privileges in life. It is something that I will never, ever regret. There's much more of this world I'd like to see and experience, but if and when I do so, I *know* that I will ever and always be tethered to my *Sense of Place.*

A Sense of Place
(May 1998)

Where are you from? Where grow your roots?
Neither here, nor there, neither hither nor yon?
Like Zephyr, have you neither track nor trace?
Not so I, for I have a sense of place.
Place is a valley, fairest daughter of Grassy Ridge and
Yellow Bald.
Cruel and kind, distant and near, a strange lover is she.
She wrings my heart with scorn and grace;
But I love her still, for she is my sense of place.
Place is the gallery where the memories hang;
The chief volume that tells my tale;

The canvas that captures my face.
Oh! the images that cling to this sense of place!
Farewell forever, fair fields, cold waters, mystic heights!
She beckons and calls like some old forlorn tune;
Pointing toward the hillside where sleeps my kindred race.
Lay me there to rest, I pray, in the bosom of my
sense of place.

Chapter 2: Valley, North Carolina

Place, *my* place, is a rather insignificant-looking dot on a North Carolina map. For the uninitiated, I often have to start with Asheville, Boone, or even Charlotte to help them locate it. When trying to explain where I'm from, the response is usually, and I will add *understandably*, a flat-line brain wave indicator. "Avery County?" I'll ask, "do you know where that is?" Flat lines. "Grandfather Mountain? The ski slopes—Beech Mountain, Sugar Mountain?" Light bulbs!

Avery County is the youngest of North Carolina's one hundred counties. It was founded in 1911, when my Great Grandfather Garfield was 29 years of age. It was founded the same year my maternal grandmother was born, and a year before the Titanic sank. It borders Carter County, Tennessee to the west. Avery is the third northwestern-most county in North Carolina. It's about a hundred miles northwest of Charlotte, seventy miles northeast of Asheville, and about five hundred miles from everywhere else. It's hard or next to impossible to get there from here or anywhere else.

Roaring Creek is accessed by vehicular traffic only from the south, off U.S. Highway 19-E. It is located about fifteen miles southwest of Newland, the county seat. Up until about fifty years ago, my folks' mailing address was simply *Route 1 Newland*, without any other identifying house or road numbers. The closest decent sized grocery stores are in Banner Elk, Newland, and Spruce Pine, each close to fifteen to twenty miles away.

At one time, and I don't know for how long, Roaring Creek was named *Roan Creek*. Seeing how some of the smaller streams on Roaring Creek have their headwaters just under the Roan Highlands complex, that makes sense. There's also a good reason why it was once called *Valley*. Even doing an online search, it is still as of this writing, sometimes designated *Valley* in online maps. It's hard to imagine now, but at one time, Valley, North Carolina even had its own post office. I have some old cards and letters stamped with the Valley postmark.

On Valley's northwestern border, the 6189-foot Grassy Ridge Bald, one of the tallest peaks east of the Mississippi, maintains a proud vigil. To the east, Big Yellow Mountain, at 5460 feet, with Big Hump Mountain watching over her shoulder, casts a watchful eye over the sons and daughters of the valley.

The name to which Place now answers is simply *Roaring Creek*. Politically, it is designated *Roaring Creek Township*. Much to my delight, even one of those popular talking/listening gadgets can give us the weather report for Roaring Creek Township. We don't talk much to ours anymore by the way, because it knows way too much, and tells everything it hears. For a long time, it resided safely and solitarily in an undisclosed location. It is currently out on good behavior, but remains so on probation.

I don't know if the native inhabitants of Roaring Creek had any mythical stories about the creation of the valley or not (I'm betting they did), but I would at least like to imagine that I know how it happened. Taoism, one of several Asian philosophies/religions, gave us the concepts of Yin and Yang. As an over-simplified explanation, Taoism (sometimes spelled Daoism) is a religion/philosophy of complementary opposites—i.e., life is predicated on opposite, yet equal, complementary principles—light and dark; good and evil; aggressive and passive; etc. As expected, it also includes male and female—opposite, equal, and yet complementary. In Taoism, male is rough, pointed, aggressive; female is soft, rounded, passive. Peacemaker that I try to be, I know some are thinking "Hold on here! I know *lots* of passive males and *lots* of aggressive females!" Of course, but these are *general* principles from Taoism. I would tell you to take it up with Lao Tzu (also spelled Laozi/Lao-Tze), the founder, but he died about four hundred years or so before Christ.

In my 21st Century mythological re-creation, I'd like to think that Grassy Ridge is male, and that Big Yellow is female. Grassy Ridge is larger and more rugged than Big Yellow, and pointed at its apex. Big Yellow, the female counterpart, has voluptuous curves and dips, and is rounder, and softer than Grassy Ridge. I think that eons ago, Grassy Ridge and Big Yellow made passionate love, and their offspring is Roaring Creek Valley. Oh, how they doted on that gorgeous valley, their pride and joy, their one and only child, and a prodigy at that!

I grew up in a place, where, for 150 years, change has occurred in snail-like increments. It's not so much a place that Time forgot, but one of which Time was either largely unaware or simply chose to ignore. Far from the restless, raucous influence of asphalt-covered "civilization," Roaring Creek, is cradled by the very hand of God, between the vast fertile ridges of the Blue Ridge Mountains. East Tennesseans, whose easternmost border in Carter County touches the valley, swear that kudzu and western North Carolinians are might nigh about to take over their part of the country!

The Yellow Mountain Gap, on the valley's westernmost border, was an important passage for the Overmountain Men in 1780. They had rendezvoused at Sycamore Shoals, in what is now Elizabethton, Tennessee. They marched up Hampton Creek in Roan Mountain, Tennessee, and over the mountain, through the Yellow Mountain Gap, down the valley, and on to a decisive battle at King's Mountain, South Carolina.

There's no mystery as to why Place is now called *Roaring Creek*. The valley is divided by a sizeable stream that runs a total of about five miles or so. The main branch takes its headwaters near the Yellow Mountain Gap, and about a mile down the valley is joined by the frigid waters of Elk Hollow. In addition to some smaller, lesser-known branches, three other named creeks and or branches join the main artery—Jerry's Creek (largest of the three), Martin's Branch, and Mollie's Branch. On its roaring, roiling, relentless journey to the sea, Roaring Creek winds and finds its way to Toe River. Toe River eventually morphs into the scenic and notorious Nolichucky, watery executioner of hundreds of unfortunate souls.

There are fine nuances between rivers, creeks, and branches that any true Creeker would know. They're nuanced in terms of size. Going in reverse order would be the easiest way to explain it. A river is larger than a creek. A creek is larger than a branch. Branches are formed by the overflow of springs. Springs are the source of all streams. Abundant rain, of which the Valley usually gets plenty, keeps the majority of the springs flowing year-round.

Roaring Creek is considered to be one of America's most scenic valleys. Admittedly, I'm biased, but at least I'm not the only one who thinks that. A real estate agent recently asked me if, while I was growing up on Roaring Creek, I ever took its beauty for granted. I was immensely gratified and proud to say without a nanosecond's hesitation that I never did, and I certainly don't now. I appreciated it as a child, and even more so as an adult.

From the summer of 1979, immediately following high school graduation, until the summer of 1982, I lived in Greenville, South Carolina. I moved to Greenville to attend a small Bible college. Upstate South Carolina is a nice area, and has seen tremendous growth and prosperity over the past few decades. Greenville is about a two and a half—three-hour drive from Roaring Creek.

I'm not too big and tough to admit that that brief three-year period seemed more like thirteen years rather than three. I was almost constantly homesick. Naturally a homebody, I'd never been out on my own, never paid rent or a utility bill, and had never worked a public job. With all three of those quickly becoming reality after my southward migration, life actually went very well. It turned out to be a significant rite of passage into adulthood. A friend told me just before I left in 1979 that I'd be back in six months. Well, I wasn't, but I sure wanted to be, and a couple of times he almost proved himself prophetic.

On the fateful late-June day when I left the safe womb of Roaring Creek for Greenville, I packed nearly everything I had, both boxes of it. I tossed my belongings into the back of a 1978 brown Subaru hatchback, with beige and orange stripes, and white spoke steel rims. I wound my way down Roaring Creek Road, onto Highway 19-E South; then onto Highway 194 in Ingalls; onto Highway 221, between Linville and Altamont; down through the North Cove; Marion; and Rutherfordton.

Not far out of Rutherfordton, I crossed the South Carolina state line. Right after Chesnee, South Carolina, and then near Spartanburg, I hit I-85 South. At that point, it was getting serious. I was now officially in Tiger and Gamecock country. No Carolina blue or NC State red were anywhere to be seen, just lots of Clemson orange and University of South Carolina garnet. I passed sprawling peach orchards, and saw signs advertising produce stands, boiled peanuts, and hickory-smoked pork barbeque.

I soon found steady employment, my very first stint as a real, public employee. At a BI-LO supermarket, a couple of miles from my tiny single-wide trailer, I became a food and dry goods containment specialist, aka "a bag boy." I pretty much ate off of the surprisingly good tip money. I worked during the day, and come August through May, went to class four nights a week.

My last year of Bible college was particularly challenging, as I had a new third-shift job at a factory that produced vitamins and minerals. That midnight to 8 AM shift was torture for me, even as a twenty-year old. If I tried to do that now, it'd probably be a death sentence. The good Lord just didn't wire my constitution up in such a way as not to go to bed when normal people do.

For at least a year, my car reeked of the overpowering, pungent scent of vitamin B, and probably several other vitamins and minerals. The scent of the B vitamins overwhelmed the others. At least my car and I stayed healthy. Apparently, all those vitamins and minerals kept us both from breaking down. I did learn that if you get ascorbic acid (one of the forms of vitamin C) on leather boots or sneakers, and then get them wet, it'll eat them up like battery acid. I'm no chemist, but I'll bet that's partly why it's called ascorbic *acid*.

For three years, almost every weekend, come Friday (and, Lord forgive me, sometimes skipping a class or three on Friday night), I'd gas up that little brown Subaru and head for the blue hills of home. I couldn't get there fast enough.

Upstate South Carolina has some hills and mountains, some really nice ones actually. Caesar's Head, not far from Traveler's Rest, off Highway 25, is breathtaking. Greenville itself sparkles beneath the vigilant eye of Paris Mountain. But it wasn't home. Never was. It was a three-year endurance test, a stopping place, an important bend in the road in my personal journey. Looking back, I think I honestly cared more about just making it back home than I did the learning experience of formal schooling. But I certainly can't say that I regret it.

On my weekly pilgrimage back home, I would usually re-trace the same steps as when I initially moved to South

Carolina. Sometimes I'd go home via a more direct, northern route through the South Carolina mountains; on into Hendersonville, North Carolina; then Asheville; eventually hitting good old 19-E on the northwest edge of Asheville; then on into Burnsville; Spruce Pine; finally turning left onto Roaring Creek Road. Regardless of the route I chose, all roads eventually led me back to Roaring Creek.

The most cherished memory I have of heading home for the weekend was one that occurred predictably and repeatedly. On my usual Friday sojourn back to Roaring Creek, I'd uneventfully drive up I-85 for a good thirty-five to forty-five minutes, just humdrum driving through the ever-so-slightly rolling hills of the Upstate. If it was still daylight with decent visibility, *it* would happen. Every. Single. Time. Just beyond Chesnee, South Carolina, not far out of Rutherfordton, North Carolina, there it was! Peering with intensity toward the Northwest, as far as my bespectacled eyes would allow, I'd see that unmistakable jagged, blue horizon. No more monotonous rolling hills of the piedmont, but rather my beloved Blue Ridge Mountains. They were beckoning, calling, and waving at me like a lover from whom I'd been separated by just a little over 100 miles. I'm positive that my heart would always skip a beat, and I'd get a lump in my throat. Suddenly, the drab curtains of the mostly unspectacular landscape were pushed aside, revealing the happy distant welcome of home, close enough to see, but not quite close enough to touch.

Somewhere, way over yonder, within the masterpiece of that blue fabric, was nothing more than a narrow crease, a mere wrinkle, a place where Father Time walked a little more slowly, but one which made my heart beat a little faster. I would soon leave my temporary confinement behind, even if for only a day or two. On that day, and every day that I made the pilgrimage,

I tried my hardest to be back home on Roaring Creek before dark.

Chapter 3: Whence Came the Creekers?

The teacher in me can't resist commencing at least one chapter with a quiz. You won't even need a half sheet of paper. Here's the True/False one-question quiz, and you either make 100 or 0. Ready? Here you go: "*Hillbilly, Redneck, and Southern Appalachian Highlanders* are all equivalent terms, describing the same people group." It's a harder question than you might think. You can't change your answer. Don't cheat by reading the next line. The answer is... an unequivocal *False*.

I'll start with the trickiest and slipperiest of that trio of terms, *Hillbilly*. Sometimes it is used as a self-identifier (I myself have employed it, and still do from time to time). In some contexts, however, *Hillbilly* is a derogatory term, used by those who view Southern Appalachian Highlanders essentially as a bunch of thoroughly inbred, feuding, moonshining, ignoramuses, resembling the casts in stereotyped movies or TV shows. *Hillbilly* is one of those terms the *we* can use to describe *us*, but if used by outsiders, it can be deemed offensive, and is probably being used condescendingly. It is indeed a slippery identifier, one whose meaning is determined by those using it, and by context.

Redneck is a term most definitely not relegated to the Southern Appalachian Highlands or even the South in general. There are rednecks that live in Berkeley, Boise, Brooklyn, and Boston. *Redneck*, as it is currently used in our vernacular, refers more to a bigoted, narrow, devil-may-care rebel mentality and mindset, rather than to the demographic of a particular location. To be sure, *redneck* is an Americana sub-culture.

Let's move on, but let's at least get this much right. Historically, the people in the part of the country of which I write, and from whom I derive, are *Southern Appalachian*

Highlanders. Again, to keep it fair and honest, some *do indeed* self-identify as hillbillies, or rednecks, or both, but let's not confuse the finer nuances. Those of us who are aware of our Southern Appalachian heritage usually live, act, and think better than our often-undeserved reputations and misconceptions.

To the best of my knowledge, the only complete printed book of anything approximating a *specific* history of Roaring Creek was a small, pamphlet-size, unpublished booklet written in 1975 by my Great Grandfather, Rev. Garfield Hughes. There are numerous newspaper articles, blog posts, and glancing historical references to Roaring Creek, but, once again, to the best of my knowledge, there is no published, complete, specific history. Neither is this book a *complete* history, not by a long shot.

I gleaned a few things from "Grandpa 'Field" before his death in 1979 at age 97. Others have pursued interests that are more genealogical in nature, and less historically slanted. I know of at least one publication of local stories. Some, like the late Horton Cooper, wrote brief histories of Avery County, and a few recent ones have been produced as well.

Roaring Creek was a perfectly logical choice for those early settlers whose roots were in the British Isles, particularly the Scottish Highlands. Roaring Creek Valley normally receives abundant rain, and is well watered by the four major creeks that converge into one. Roaring Creek is rocky, rugged, mountainous, and features cold winters, short springs, and mild summers. In the Roan Highlands, a curious chain of natural balds, a Scottish Highlander would have felt right at home. Conversely, I've never traveled to the British Isles, but I think this would partly explain why I have such a hankering to go. I'm told that the Roan Highlands were formed during the last

Ice Age, and that you'd have to go as far north as Canada to find some of the same flora.

In 2001, I had the incredible privilege of talking with the now-deceased Mrs. Zora Green, one of our oldest Roaring Creek residents at the time. She was one of the last of the old-time local historians. She had several of her articles printed in some of the weekly county papers. Zora was a sharp-witted, humble, gracious lady, who possessed a gift of elegant writing. One of my many regrets in life, is that I waited so long to sit a spell with her, and glean from her treasure chest of knowledge and memory. Gaining appreciation for what we have is a major peak to cross toward maturity. I just wish that it didn't take us so confounded long to realize that.

One of the biggest questions that I've had about we who became the sons and daughters of Roaring Creek has never been answered to my complete satisfaction. The question concerns our *exact* origin. Even Ms. Zora couldn't give me a completely satisfactory answer. She did, however, turn over an unfamiliar stone, and reveal the name of a man named Jones Hughes. Jones, possibly also known by other names, presumably came from Louisiana. It wasn't until 2020 that I learned from a distant cousin and Hughes genealogist, Robin Kelly, that the Louisiana connection, particularly the port of New Orleans, was an important link to my ancestry.

Of course, I do know, as others have pointed out, that the overwhelming majority of the Southern Appalachian Highlanders came from Scotland and Ireland. They were known as "Scot-Irish." There were some other European roots such as German, but the Scot-Irish were predominant. My name, Hughes, the same as Roaring Creek's first white settler, my Great, Great, Great Grandfather Jeremiah "Jerry" Hughes (1810—1893), is Welsh. So, once again, for me personally, that still begs the question: *which one* of the British Isles? Scotland? Ireland? Wales? England?

Hughes, in its various formats (Hughs, McHugh, etc.), is a quite common name in the British Isles. The more I read and learn through the painstaking efforts of others, who are far more diligent and patient in these matters than I, the more I am convinced that the Hughes story begins in Wales. I say that with not a little uncertainty. More on that d'rectly. The whole genealogical research thing would be just way too frustrating for my short attention span.

One recent Christmas gift from my wife was one of those kits that allows you to trace your ancestral roots. To absolutely no one's surprise, the results showed that something like 97% of my DNA was linked to the British Isles. I was surprised however—not disappointed, just surprised—that a tiny fraction of my DNA came from Mali. "Where's that?" I've sometimes been asked. Mali is in west Africa, if you're not certain as to where I'm referring. Being as white as a ghost, I dismissed it as a fluke. Now that I know what I know, I don't think it was a fluke at all.

In my half-hearted attempt to trace my ancestral roots, the waters have cleared somewhat for me. Again, that has precious little to do with my efforts. The family history frequently gets confused because sometimes the same person will have two different names, or there will be two or more different people with the same name. E.g., within a relatively small radius of Roaring Creek, there were two gentlemen named Jeremiah Hughes; there were two named Garfield Hughes; two or more were named Bill Hughes. Sometimes a name will also have multiple spellings.

Not long ago, I had the privilege of meeting virtually with Robin Kelly, whom I mentioned earlier. Robin has done extensive DNA research on the various Hughes clans. The obvious advantage in Robin's approach is that his research is scientific, and not based merely on hearsay or hazy records. At his behest, I'll share part of an unpublished piece he wrote entitled *Loafing with the Hughes's of Roaring Creek*. After listing the most well-known Hughes clans, Robin states:

> *There may be others, but these are the most well-known Hughes's of our area. A clan is a family with unique DNA. If you don't see a group listed, then I don't know about them and they haven't registered a test and it would good if they did. We have relatives missing. There are a lot of Hughes families, as 23% of Welsh surnames is Hughes.*
>
> *The way you track the clans is through the DNA of the man of the family, and it doesn't change from father to son. In this way you can find your people hundreds of years later and then start filling in the blanks as you prove ancestors.*

Something else that Robin mentioned was the existence of a mysterious lady named Sirelda Minarca. Remember my New Orleans and Mali references earlier? Many folks in my area love to claim native American heritage, and in many cases, there absolutely are legitimate claims to that heritage. What Robin figured out is that Ms. Minarca was very likely *not* native American, but Caribbean. The Caribbean was one of the areas to which slaves from west Africa were brought.

I'll leave the hunt for ancestry to the care of abler hands, but of this much I am absolutely certain: it is Jeremiah "Jerry" Hughes (1810—1893) who is credited as being our founding father, who first came to Roaring Creek in 1861. Jerry was the son of a Bill Hughes, and his mother was native American.

A lanky, ambitious Southern Highlander, Jerry crossed the mountain from the head of Cane Creek, in what is now Mitchell County, North Carolina, before there was any such county as Avery. He became the first white settler of the valley that has had three different names. Avery County, originally part of the counties of Watauga, Caldwell, and Mitchell, was not founded until 1911, eighteen years after Jerry died. Cane Creek and Roaring Creek are literally separated by a single ridge. After the Civil War broke out, Jerry went back to the head of Cane Creek, and stayed there until 1865.

In my Great Grandfather's written account, Jerry bought 500 acres of land at $1.00 an acre, and erected a cabin way up what is now known as Jerry's Creek. He is buried in Hughes Cemetery, about 1 ½ miles up Jerry's Creek, one of the hollows comprising Roaring Creek community. Jerry fathered thirteen children, with his progeny being responsible for the overwhelming majority of the Creekers.

Jeremiah sounds like an interesting character from what little I've been told. Apparently, Great, Great, Great Grandfather Jerry had no concept of how wealthy he could have been just in mineral rights and timber alone. His interests, however, were hunting, fishing, and trailblazing. The wild game, fish, and grazing land was what piqued his interest in Roaring Creek Valley to begin with.

I didn't realize this for a very long time, but Jerry is responsible for the founding of Roaring Creek Missionary Baptist Church in 1871. In a later chapter on religion, I refer to this once again. In my Great Grandfather's unpublished written account, penned in 1975, it happened via the following chain of events, which I have quoted below exactly as written by Grandpa 'Field. Brackets are mine for purposes of clarification. He wrote:

He [Jeremiah] *had to take his corn across the mountain over on Little Rock Creek to get it growned. So in the summer of 1871, he decided to put himself a grist mill so he went got the old man George Cook to come and built him a Jub wheel. Cook was a Baptist Preacher. By that time there had moved in the valley about five families. So grandfather and Cook decided to have them a weeks meeting. So they did get enough members to organize a Baptist Church, 104 years ago at this time* [1975]*, so grandfather Jerry is the Father of the Roaring Creek Baptist Church.*

Both of my parents were Hughes's. Full disclosure: yes, they are distantly related. A telemarketer, whose offer I accepted, whatever it was that she was selling, asked for my mother's maiden name. Upon telling her that it was "Hughes," I then gave her a good laugh by telling her that I didn't know if that made me inbred or thoroughbred! We'll say thoroughbred. Confession may be good for one's soul, but it can be bad for one's reputation.

As you would probably guess, most of the residents of Roaring Creek to this day are Hughes's. We have several other assorted surnames: Buchanan, Burleson, Calhoun, English, Greene, Hicks, Hoilman, Hopson, King, McKinney, Oaks, Webb, Young, and a smattering of others. I'm related to most of them too. Jerry Hughes had a big family.

As indicated, my mother's line descended from Jerry's line. Her mother, Hazel, was an Oaks, and Grandma Hazel's mother was a Hughes. The Oaks line entered the Valley via Charles Oaks, also known as Pap. Around the turn of the Twentieth Century, he came to Roaring Creek from the coal mines of Kentucky to work in the iron ore mines in nearby Cranberry.

He must've drunk the water on Roaring Creek, because he married Great Grandma Ebbie, and settled on the Creek.

I don't know nearly as much about my daddy's side of the family as I do my mother's. His mother was the daughter of Sam King. I'm a little hazy as to his origin. Not long ago, I saw a photograph of Sam, and it partially explains why the Kings are such a tall, handsome people. Sam looked as if his photo had been taken on the set of an old western movie. With his broad-brimmed hat and thick moustache, he looked every bit the part of a Wild West lawman or maybe even a Wild West gunslinger.

On the other hand, my paternal grandfather, Robert, descended from… yep, you guessed it… Jerry. Mercifully, Grandpa Rob's mother, Laura, was a McKinney.

In 1780, a ragtag, mad-as-hell, "amateur" militia marched down Roaring Creek Valley, en route to one of the most crucial battles of the Revolutionary War. This ragged, rugged army consisted of farmers and frontiersmen, who also happened to be ferocious fighters. They were known as the Overmountain Men. Given their toughness, their skill in close combat, their stamina, and their superb marksmanship, they simply and decisively overwhelmed General Ferguson and the Loyalists in a rout. Their date with destiny occurred at Kings Mountain, then located in South Carolina, eighty-one years before Jerry crossed the mountain.

The early settlers in Roaring Creek Valley were cut out of the same cloth as the Overmountain Men. Had the Valley been settled in 1780, without a doubt, the men would've slung their muskets over their shoulders, and joined in the 330-mile march.

Creekers are tough, but tender; independent, but generous; different, but authentic. Creekers are rarely large in physical stature, but are gigantic in their ability to persevere. Very few are well educated, but almost all possess graduate degrees in practical knowledge. Few Creekers are people of means, but they are wealthy in terms of place, of family, of simple pleasures, of contentment. The Preacher said it far better than I can even begin to approximate:

I know that there is nothing better for people than to be happy and to do good while they live. That each of them may eat and drink, and find satisfaction in all their toil—this is the gift of God (Ecclesiastes 3:12-13, NIV).

Chapter 4: The Family Tree Trunk

In some ways, there wasn't a great deal about my upbringing that was very remarkable for the area we were in and the era in which we lived. It was no doubt remarkable relative to most of the country, but not so much to the immediate area. Change came to Roaring Creek considerably more slowly than to other parts of the country, the state, and in some respects, even to my home county. The local culture, in my formative years, was rather homogenous. I'm a baby boomer who grew up in a lower middle-class, nuclear family. We were as country as cornbread, and rural with a capital *R*.

Often, I find myself saying that I don't really have a family tree, just a family trunk. It always gets a laugh. I laugh along, except I know that it's not really a joke.

Very much in keeping with the area, my father I called *daddy*, and my mother I called *mommy*. Lots of folks back home still do that. Daddy was the youngest of three, and mommy was the eldest of six. As I began to gain a better understanding of human psychology, their relationship made more sense to me.

With a terrific sense of humor, daddy could be lighthearted, nonchalant, and could've struck up a conversation with a fence post—stereotypical last-born traits. Mommy was serious as a judge, intense, and couldn't have told a joke if her life had depended on it. She projected a very pleasant, easy, calm demeanor, similar to a duck: seemingly sitting serenely in a pond, but paddling furiously beneath.

I'm certainly no psychologist, but I've no doubt that daddy and mommy's personality traits were dictated partly by birth order and partly by genetics. My thinking has evolved to the point that I firmly believe that nature trumps nurture in *most* cases.

Mommy was definitely the Alpha in the relationship and in the home. She kept daddy on the straight and narrow. Don't misunderstand at this point: daddy was very much a man's man, not one to be pushed around and lead like a bull with a nose ring, but his leadership and managerial abilities were not nearly as pronounced as mommy's. Opposites attract, so they say, and in many ways, they were exactly that.

When they were first married, daddy's favorite hobby was going to Newland on Saturday nights and looking for fights. A little firewater would usually be thrown into the mix as well. On one such Saturday evening, mommy told him that if he went to Newland that night, she wouldn't be there when he returned. He did not go to Newland that night, nor, to my knowledge, did he ever go to Newland again to look for fights. A wise man was he.

Self-reliant, duty-driven, and very Stoic in the face of adversity, my parents were tough, resilient people. On the other hand, they would do anything they could for other people, never expecting anything in return.

One Fall Sunday morning in 1977, my mother left for work en route to Cannon Memorial Hospital in Banner Elk, where she worked as a registered nurse. Five minutes or so after she left, daddy got a phone call. He came and got me out of bed early. He said "Pauline has turned her car over. Me, and you, and Clyde [mommy's brother] have to go and roll her car back over."

The three of us arrived on the scene, only a mile from our house. Fortunately, mommy wasn't injured at all. I have no idea how it happened on that relatively straight stretch of road, but she went off the right shoulder, hit the embankment, and rolled her yellow 4X4 Subaru hatchback onto its left side. Daddy, Uncle Clyde, and I gave the car a push and righted it. The car sustained very minimal damage. Mommy got back in under the wheel, turned the ignition key, and the little hatchback fired right up, and away to work she went. It was her duty. Knowing her as I did, I feel sure that she was probably more concerned about the possibility of being late for work than rolling her car. My parents were tough, resilient people.

My maternal and paternal grandparents were similar in many respects, but quite different in others. My maternal grandparents showed very little outward affection. My paternal grandparents, on the other hand, were very affectionate, and had no qualms with saying "I love you," and giving hugs and kisses. The traits of the maternal grandparents prevailed in our home, at least up until about the early 1980's.

My mother, affectionate in her own way and on her own terms, never signed a card or specifically verbalized, "I love you." It was, "Love you." I have absolutely no right to judge her for that, because that was at least a notch or three above her formative environment.

Paternal grandparents, Grandpa Rob and Grandma Nell, who lived 1/10 of a mile below us, never owned a motor vehicle. Too, I can vividly remember in my lifetime that they had an old-fashioned outhouse, not installing an indoor toilet until sometime in the late 1960's.

Grandpa Rob was a small man, tough as leather, maybe 5'6", and about 135 pounds. It was absolutely nothing for him to walk to Banner Elk and back (about a 30-mile round trip), or walk to a store in closer proximity, carrying a 100-pound sack of livestock feed across his shoulders. He did hitch a few rides along his pedestrian routes.

Grandpa Rob had a couple of cut-off fingers that he would regularly use to bore into the side of my head. Yes, it hurt. A lot. But it was his way of expressing male rough-housing affection. Word had it that he was once trimming a tree and sawed off the limb he was sitting on. Note to self: always take note of where you're sitting if you plan to trim a tree.

Grandma Nell was sharp as a tack. Her memory and ability to recall were phenomenal. She could tell you everyone's birthday, anniversary, and date of death. She was a reader, a thinker, and had a great sense of humor. One the funniest stories I remember from Grandma Nell was the one she told me about a certain cemetery. She said that there was this particular cemetery, and if you went there at midnight and hollered "What are you doing?" the deceased residents would say, "Nothing." It took me a little while, but I finally got it.

The tendency to change was not a prominent trait in Grandma Nell, or for that part, most of the folks from her generation. She never saw the ocean, and didn't want to, because, in her words, "Full water scares me." She also never put up a Christmas tree. Why? Because she had never put one up before, and she wasn't going to start it. Her one Christmas decoration was a lonely, pitiful sprig of plastic holly, with a few red plastic berries, attached to an aluminum foil-wrapped bell. Grandma Nell was clearly a minimalist.

Maternal grandparents, Grandpa Jack and Grandma Hazel, who lived 1/10 mile above us, availed themselves of more technological advancements than did Grandpa Rob and Grandma Nell. They used an oil stove for heat, unlike Grandpa Rob and Grandma Nell, who burned wood throughout my lifetime. Grandpa Jack liked vehicles, and owned several different cars and trucks that I can remember. Grandpa Jack was a kindhearted, gentle soul, who lived his life quietly and modestly. He was an excellent manager of his very meager means. At the time of his death in 1994, he drew somewhere in the neighborhood of $300 a month Social Security. But he and Grandma Hazel always had plenty of food, clean clothes, and all the necessary comforts of home.

Grandma Hazel became like a second mother to me. Unlike many of the women in the community from my mother's generation, my mother worked, and so I stayed up at Granny Hazel's. Grandma Hazel suffered from depression throughout most of her life, being institutionalized for a brief period, after the birth of her sixth and last child, my Aunt Sandra. She did what all the older ladies in the community did—reared her children, cooked, cleaned, sewed, raised a garden, quilted, and watched soap operas religiously Monday through Friday.

Saturdays were different from other days for Grandma Hazel and family, because *Mid-Atlantic Championship Wrestling, Hee Haw*, and the *Grand Old Opry* were broadcast on their TV that picked up three channels, just as ours did. I'm not sure how many of the senior ladies in the community were into watching professional wrestling. Perhaps some were closet fans, but it was like a cult following among many back home. To say that they got worked up over it, was an understatement.

It's so ironic to me that Grandma Hazel was a splendid cook, but absolutely hated cooking. She seemed genuinely perturbed that people could eat so much. Given a choice, she would've subsisted on sugar. The only complaint that I ever heard about her cooking came from daddy. He said more than once that Grandma Hazel just didn't bake enough bread!

Great Grandfather, Rev. Garfield Hughes, a pillar in the community, lived with my maternal grandparents, Grandpa Jack and Grandma Hazel. Grandpa Jack was his only son. Grandpa 'Field, as we called him, was twice widowed, and lived to be 97. One of the oddest things in my mother's family was that they referred to their Grandfather Garfield as "daddy," and to their father by his first name, Jack. It wasn't a respect issue at all, just a family oddity.

Daddy and mommy were part of the Great Depression-World War II generation. There's a reason theirs is sometimes referred to as the *Greatest Generation*. They exemplified that reason. They were frugal almost to a fault, but they knew how make do with what they had, worked like mules, and didn't expect to be handed anything for nothing.

World War II ended in August 1945, and my parents were married in October of that year, October 31 to be exact. Daddy had served honorably in the U.S. Marine Corps, and had a short leave before he would be discharged a few months later. They could've waited or gone ahead and tied the knot during that short leave. They opted for the latter. Thus, the unusual wedding anniversary. It was one day after daddy turned 23, and seven weeks before mommy would turn 19.

The Great Depression had finally come to a merciful end, the war was over, and optimism was trending high across the land. It wouldn't be long before the George and Pauline babies started arriving. The first was in 1946. His name was George Jason Hughes, Jr. Junior died from complications during childbirth. George, Jr. was my eldest brother, and the first of two brothers whom I'll never meet in this life.

In 1947, brother Larry was born. By default, he became heir to the title of eldest child. He wouldn't be alone for long, because in 1949, along came little brother Keith. Yet another sad story there.

Keith contracted pneumonia, which, in our 21st Century, doesn't sound too serious, but in the remote mountains of western North Carolina in the early 1950's, it was a very critical illness. Whether viral or bacterial pneumonia, I don't know, but it was serious.

Keith had begged my mother to put up their Christmas tree during the Christmas season of 1953. For whatever reasons, she didn't. Keith died December 14, 1953, eleven days before Christmas. Mommy and daddy had already bought him a little red wagon as a Christmas gift. I would be a grown man before

I learned why mommy seemed to wait so long before putting up a Christmas tree. She resolutely refused to do so until *after* December 14. Now I understand better the shoes in which she walked.

The same year that Keith died, three months prior, Pamela was born. She looked like my handsome daddy spat her out of his mouth. In 1955, mommy and daddy would have a second consecutive girl, Donna. It seems that Donna was blown in by the winds of March, and every bit as tempestuous!

Over five years passed, and in December 1960, yours truly was hatched. Given how relatively stair-stepped my other siblings had been in their birth order, I'm fairly certain that I should have been named *Oops*. I was born nine months after the legendary, record snowfall of March 1960. I assume that there wasn't much outside work to be done that March.

I was generally terrified of my two sisters. I was convinced that, with enough provocation, they would have tossed me over the embankment, just beyond the top of the driveway, into the beech grove, where the witch lived. They said there was a witch that lived down there, so obviously, it had to be true. Many times, after dark, coming back from Grandma Hazel's and Grandpa Jack's house, I had to walk past that beech grove. There were a few times that I could have sworn that I felt that witch's cold, putrid breath on the back of my neck. Thankfully, I was just a step or two faster.

I can remember a few scarce events all the way back to when I was three years old. For example, I remember my Uncle Jerry and Aunt Sandra getting married. For reasons I probably don't want to remember, I recall a red cherry tree that stood in the front yard, just a few feet from the house. My mother used to break limbs off that tree and wear us out when we needed it, which seemed to be fairly regularly. I also have a vague memory of daddy remodeling our old house.

Sometime in 1955, the same year that Donna was born, daddy and mommy bought the house of Fate Singleton. It was a tiny house of maybe 800 square feet, but not exceptionally small for our area. The house came with twenty-nine acres of land. For the staggering sum of $1500.00, they were now the proud owners of twenty-nine acres and the house I grew up in, and eventually inherited.

In the early 1960's, daddy undertook a significant remodeling project of the house, and added two bedrooms and a cellar to the South-facing end. The finished product was a house of around 1100 square feet. I heard daddy say more than once, "Whenever you remodel a' old house, it's still a' old house when ye git done!" Truer words were never spoken.

The 1950's and 1960's created a number of tectonic shifts in the cultural landscape. For example, it became acceptable for mothers to be employed outside the home. My mother was one of the few working mothers there on the Creek during that era. She wasn't trying to make a statement or be stylish. She did what she had to do for the sake of her family. She never did anything casually, and was a very hard worker. The first job that I remember her having was as a check-out clerk, stock woman, and all-around go-getter at R.S. Burleson's General Store. The store was in the Senia community, about three miles from our house. Everyone knew the store simply as Bob's Store, which stood about two hundred and fifty yards from Erwin's Grocery Store. Both structures still stand today, but neither is in operation. My family shopped at both stores.

One of my favorite memories is frequently going into Bob's Store and having cousin Edgar Hughes, a distant cousin and employee at Bob's, make me a thick-cut bologna sandwich on white bread, slathered with mayonnaise. Then I'd go grab an ice-cold Mountain Dew out of one of those old-timey drink boxes. If I were to find a genie in a lamp, I'd use one of my three wishes to be able to go back and do that again.

The first job that I recall daddy having in my lifetime was as a second-shift laborer at the Tarheel Mica Company in nearby Plumtree. Before that, he had done some logging up in Maryland and other areas, and had worked at sawmills. He was always a very hard, dependable worker. The Tarheel made all sorts of mica-based products. It seems that nearly half of Roaring Creek was employed at the Tarheel. The Tarheel had a quitting-time whistle that could be clearly and easily heard on a clear day, all the way up Roaring Creek, six miles away.

In retrospect, I'm sure that daddy had low self-esteem, and lacked confidence in his potential. Again, that was part and parcel of the culture. It was simply understood, unspoken, and unwritten that you accept your lot in life, get over it, and get on with it. End of story. At least it was how the story ended for most.

Daddy could do so many things so well, but I don't think he truly saw himself for the man he was and could've been. He hid it pretty well to others, with his easy demeanor and sense of humor. He, I think, like a lot of the men in our community, epitomized Thoreau's famous line in that they lived "...*lives of quiet desperation.*"

Here's the silver lining: daddy was content being who he was. Especially in his waning years, he was happy, loved life, and seized the day. Who could criticize that? Just a month or two after he turned sixty-two, he retired from Henredon Furniture. I never saw anyone enjoy their well-deserved retirement any more than he.

One day, as boys are wont to do, I was prowling around in our musty, old, spider-haunted coat closet, and found a small, attractive wooden box. Of course, like an explorer finding a pirate's chest, I couldn't resist opening it. It was an architectural drafting kit of some sort. At one time, I later learned, daddy had considered becoming a draftsman.

With nary a word, that little rectangular wooden box spoke volumes. It evokes a sense of sadness for me to think that daddy's desire went no further than just a mere wish, and became no more than "…what might have been," revealed only by a pretty wooden box. Whether literally or metaphorically, I suspect that a lot of us have our own pretty wooden boxes, filled with *should haves, shouldn't haves,* and *wish I hads.*

Chapter 5: Thicker Than Water

The 1960's hit my unsuspecting parents like a wrecking ball. Other than the philosophically and culturally astute, I doubt if there were very many in their generation, on Roaring Creek or elsewhere, who were ready for the cultural convulsion that took place.

Larry was well into his teens in the 60's, with Pam and Donna not terribly far behind him in age. I, on the other hand, still in my single-digit years, had not a clue as to what was going on.

It seems that the very earth clave asunder when the Beatles made their debut on the Ed Sullivan Show back in 1964, three months after President Kennedy was assassinated. Mommy's description of Rock-N-Roll was "that hollerin' and screamin'!!!" The Beatles, of course, were fairly mild in comparison to the wave of new artists who came a little later.

The very next year, after the Beatles landed, the U.S. deployed troops to Vietnam. After that, the proverbial fan was circulating more than just air. I was too young to remember the details of those momentous events, but not too young to remember the upheavals of the next dozen years or so. The late 1960's was marked by escalating social unrest; protests; riots; the civil rights movement; the assassinations of Rev. Dr. Martin Luther King, Jr. and Bobby Kennedy; talk of communists taking over America; the race to be the first on the moon; the sexual revolution; and the hippie generation.

Combine the following elements: a cultural revolution that hit like a powerful storm; societal unrest, whose shockwaves were felt even in extremely rural areas like Roaring Creek; two teenage sisters who barely tolerated each other, and who themselves were experiencing the new Great Awakening; and two parents who were born in the 1920's, who didn't understand the turbulence of the times. That combination was something like gasoline, dry grass, and matches.

Brother Larry had joined the U.S. Marine Corps in 1966, and was, quite literally, a year later, going to Vietnam when I was going into the first grade. Understandably, being only six when Larry began his own epic journey, I have very few early memories of him. For a long time, I think Larry felt badly that he and I never grew up together. We were virtual strangers. The redeeming virtue is that in the past ten to fifteen years or so, we've actually gotten better acquainted, and discovered that we have more in common than either of us realized. We really are related! It wasn't personal, nor was it intentional. It was neither his fault nor mine. It was just biology, and irreversible circumstances.

What I do remember about Larry from my childhood, and quite vividly, is that I worshipped the very ground he walked on. With his being my big brother, and not unlike a lot of little brothers, I thought he was right up there with Gabriel the angel. What wasn't to adore? He was strong, handsome, smart, athletic (fullback, number 20, on the Cranberry High School football team), popular, charming, had a car, a motorcycle, and was and still is a gearhead who loved big bad toys that go *VROOM*! He's a lifelong and ardent subscriber to the philosophy that *loud pipes save lives.*

My personal nirvana back in the mid to late 60's was riding with Larry on the back of his blue, twin-cylinder, 160cc Honda motorcycle, despite burning my leg on the exhaust pipe. I rode with him a few times in his avocado green Mustang Mach 1, sporting big, wide, Mickey Thompson tires, and rode with him a time or two on his 900 Harley Sportster that he got a little later. That little puddle jumping Honda and that Mach 1 paled in comparison to Larry's lineup of big, muscular, earth-shaking

Harleys that would make their advent in the decades to come, along with a stable of Corvettes that would be the envy of even the slightest car buff. I get a rush just hearing the exhaust of a big Harley, or a high-powered muscle car. Maybe I'm just a wee bit of a closet gearhead myself.

One of the most significant memories of my life occurred in January 1967. I had just turned six, and it was the night Larry flew out of the Asheville regional airport, headed to Camp Pendleton in California. From Camp Pendleton, he would deploy to Vietnam, several months later.

I'm sharing this particular memory *not* to garner pity. It has actually helped me to understand one or three of my many idiosyncrasies. There is no blame being assigned, and no pity being sought, only facts and perceptions to be shared. Perception, as it is said, is reality.

On the fateful evening of Larry's flight, mommy's brother, Uncle Curt, drove the four of us—he, Larry, my mother, and me—down out of the lonely blue mountains to the tiny Asheville regional airport. Daddy was working at his second-shift job at the Tarheel Mica plant, and did not accompany the four of us. Uncle Curt was a diehard Pontiac devotee, and transported us in his 60's-something seafoam blue Catalina. I always loved Uncle Curt. He was different from the rest of the family. Dare I say, *cool*. And—God have mercy—he married Janeen, a girl from the land of Up North! I'm being facetious. I've always loved Aunt Janeen as well, who made things fun for us young goblins. Plus, she introduced me to Hungarian goulash. That sealed the deal.

If memory serves correctly, we arrived at the Asheville airport as day was transitioning to dusk. This was still in the days when you could accompany your friends and loved ones all the way to the airport boarding gate. Airport protocol was far different then from now. Goodbyes were said, and the dreaded moment of departure came. Again, I'm relying on a 50-plus year-old memory, but it seems that we were standing outside in the cool night air of mid-winter as the rumbling jet, with Larry aboard, taxied up the runway.

Somewhere, outside the terminal—standing, waiting, watching—all eyes were on that roaring jet. It's so odd what random items our gray file still pulls up so easily, but I clearly remember Uncle Curt commenting on the speed of the craft as it taxied up the runway for takeoff. He said something to the effect "He's [the pilot] up to about 90 now...." I was astounded! 90 was fast as far as I was concerned, but how did Uncle Curt know that? He just did. He knew stuff like that.

With a roar that seemed to split the very air, differentiating the invisible divide between present and future, my big brother, in that big jet plane, making a big loud noise just as he liked, soared into the ever-darkening horizon. Far, far away from the Asheville airport, and further still from our humble valley haven, a jagged, unbreachable chasm in time had been rent.

At that moment, my mother said through bitter tears, wrung from the very depths of her broken heart, "I'll never see him again!" Oh! the pathos of such a simple statement, forever penned in indigo ink on the parchment of memory. Understand, my mother rarely, I mean *rarely* as in two full moons in the same month, cried in front of others. I didn't cry, but my heart melted and ran into my little boy-sized shoes. Uncle Curt tried to console her "Now don't talk like that! He'll be back!" Larry was always her most favored child. I didn't fully understand or appreciate the pathos and the significance of that moment of course, but I knew that whatever it was that had just happened was a really big deal, and a life-changing event.

To this day, it evokes something very deep within me, and touches a part of me that will forever be sore and tender whenever I hear the blast of a departing jet. It doesn't matter if it's a large jet or smallish private jet. Eleven times out of ten, I'll tear up. Inexplicably, the same is true if I hear the deafening, grinding roar of a lumbering locomotive train. Parades do the same. Emergency sirens do the same, but I think I know the reason for that last one. That's another story. I still don't fully understand that strange emotional response mechanism, but a few of the dots that stretch across the continuum of six decades have begun to connect.

How ironic that I now reside less than a mile from a small airport that regularly hosts private jets. Strangely, like rubbernecking at a terrible car accident, I absolutely love the roar of a jet engine. If I'm out working in my yard or taking a walk down by the airport, I'll always stop what I'm doing to watch and listen as someone leaves from *here* to go wherever *there* happens to be. Whether it's a departing jet, the sight of tail lights fading in the distance, or a ship sailing over the horizon—it's all about departure—leaving *here*, going *there*. At least that's the case from where I stand.

By default, Uncles Clyde and Michael became my big brothers. They were always very good to me. I spent as much time as possible with them. Michael was married, so I didn't see as much of him until after he and his first wife divorced, but Uncle Clyde still lived at home. He didn't marry until he was in his early 40's.

Sitting between Uncle Clyde and someone else I can't recall, in the front seat of Clyde's Chevrolet sedan, I remember the exact spot on Roaring Creek Road, where Uncle Clyde gave me my first taste of beer. Admittedly, it was love at first sip. Fortunately for Uncle Clyde, my mother never found out. The fact that he lived several more decades is proof of that!

The turbulent 1960's rocked and rolled on, and we kept up with goings-on mainly via television. We had a black and white television, and could clearly pick up three stations: WBTV out of Charlotte (CBS); WCYB out of Bristol, Tennessee (NBC); and WJHL out of Johnson City, Tennessee (CBS). We could pick up a very snowy ABC station out of Asheville, provided that daddy would go upon the roof of the house and literally turn the antenna. He liked that station because they broadcast a lot of sports.

Saturday morning was cartoon day. On Sunday mornings, we watched *The Gospel Singing Jubilee,* and on Sunday nights, we'd watch *The Ed Sullivan Show, Mutual of Omaha's Wild Kingdom,* and *Disney. Lost In Space* was our Wednesday staple. Other than *Mid-Atlantic Championship Wrestling, Hee Haw, The Little Rascals, Gilligan's Island,* and several yearly airings of *The Wizard of Oz*, and an occasional *National Geographic* special, I wasn't a big TV watcher. A black and white TV that picks up three channels doesn't easily lend itself to binge watching.

WCYB probably had the most accurate weather forecast for our area, but we were CBS people who watched WBTV out of Charlotte for our regional news. At 7 PM, it was the incomparable Walter Cronkite for world news. In those days, major news figures like Mr. Cronkite, just blandly and stoically reported the news. Lordy mercy how I miss that!

Most nights I watched the evening news like an adult. The iconic Mr. Cronkite would report on Vietnam, the Viet Cong, Communists, Saigon, Laos, Cambodia, the DMZ, the Ho Chi Minh Trail, Khe Sanh, Phnom Penh, etc. They would show plane and troop icons at the bottom of the TV screen. I'd listen to reports on guerilla warfare, and the number of troop casualties. Dan Rather, who eventually succeeded Mr. Cronkite as news anchor, was an on-ground reporter during that war. It was the first war ever to be broadcast into homes.

Every night I would say my prayers. I had this blanket-coverage prayer in which I would pray for everyone in the world *except* the Viet Cong, the communists, and the devil. Although I wasn't entirely certain who the first two entities were, I nevertheless felt compelled to include that exception clause. I wanted to keep things clear between the Lord and me. By doing so, hopefully, no divine benefits would be extended to those three aforementioned entities. I suppose I must have missed that part of Holy Writ that tells us to pray for our enemies, but my assumption was that since Larry was over *there*, fighting against *them*, then I sure didn't want to offer up any prayers on their behalf.

For all practical purposes, I was an only child. I liked it that way. To this day, I derive strength and contentment from solitude. I don't like solitude 24/7 of course, but to refresh and recharge, solitude is my modus operandi. I've had many people laugh in my face upon hearing me confess to being an introvert. It's 100% true—I'm an introvert. To others, I may function and appear to be an extrovert, but that's only out of functional necessity. The people who laugh probably don't really know what an introvert is, but my name is Chris, and I am an introvert.

My goal as kid was to have fun, play, and endure school. The only parts of school that I liked were girls and recess. Up until I was around ten or eleven, somewhere around there, my waking hours were mainly spent up at Grandpa Jack's and Grandma Hazel's, my maternal grandparents. They allowed me to do pretty much anything, even dip, chew, and smoke a pipe. Not all freedom is optimum.

My number one thing was playing in and around the frog pond out behind Grandpa Jack's and Grandma Hazel's house. Occasionally, I'd be joined by cousins. Other than the brief period when the bottom of my feet cracked open with huge crevices that made my feet look like a topographical map, I had an idyllic time. I could be anybody I wanted to be, play cars, trucks, cowboys and Indians, go fishing, catch tadpoles, dam up the branch, swim in the big hole, seek and destroy girls' playhouses (Lord forgive me), build fires, skip rocks, eat, sleep, and do it all again the next day.

Some of us were born anxious. I was one of the lucky winners in that category. I had terrible separation anxiety, and to a certain extent still do. I liked my routine and my familiar surroundings. Still do. Every now and then I'd go to Spruce Pine with Grandpa Jack and Grandma Hazel. Spruce Pine proper was right at twenty miles away. Grandpa Jack barely crept down highway 19-E in his ancient car, and later his old truck. He would give me a little bit of spending money, just a few coins. Along with Grandma Hazel, I'd go to the Dime Store. Grandpa Jack usually went to the barber shop to have all three of his hairs trimmed.

In the Dime Store, I'd be over on the toy aisle, blissfully unaware that Grandma Hazel had disappeared over in the next aisle. Upon the realization that the lady whose dress I was absentmindedly tugging on, to show her something interesting that I had found, wasn't Grandma Hazel, I'd panic. It was no gradual panic, but an instantaneous, hit-the-red button kind of panic. *"Grandmaaaaa Haaazel!!!"* I'd yell to the top of my lungs. *"Whoooo!"* she'd reply, and I'd follow the sound until I found her, and the panic would subside.

It's quite ironic that I enjoyed being, functionally at least, an only child. I enjoyed being by myself in the great outdoors, but that was only in my familiar surroundings. It was really embarrassing when I was several years older, getting separated from my mother, and having to get an employee at the old Big K department store in Elizabethton, Tennessee to page her over the store's intercom. I'll never forget it: "Pauline Hughes, please come to the front of the store and get your son." It was utterly embarrassing, but I chose humiliation over separation anxiety.

Un-American as it sounds, I do *not* like baseball. I don't like to play it, watch it, or listen to games on the radio. I don't give a flying monkey's behind about ERA's, homeruns, and stolen bases. Just hear me out for a minute or two.

I have great respect for those who excel at baseball, especially those who play at the highest level. The skillset required to play at that level is incredible. Plus, I think it's a brilliantly conceived game. I have reasons though for my sour attitude.

In the early 1970's, when I was around ten, I decided to try out for a community baseball team. My fourth cousin, David Burleson, played baseball, and I caught a ride with him and his father, Howard. David was pretty good, and had a ton of experience. I had plenty enough strength and speed for my age, but I was not blessed with a surplus of hand-eye coordination, of which baseball requires an abundance.

For some reason, Coach didn't like me. At least it didn't *seem* that he did. If he did, he hid his feelings really well. Perception is reality. It couldn't have had anything to do with something I said, because Coach and I never had an actual conversation during practice. I don't remember his teaching me anything. I only remember that he was very critical of my, shall I say, *undeveloped potential.*

On a particular Saturday morning, sometime in mid-spring, all of the county little league teams assembled in Newland, our county seat, for some sort of little league parade. I was super excited. There were colorful baseball caps and uniformed players galore from various parts of the county.

I noticed that all the other boys on my team were wearing their uniforms. "Hmm," thought I, not completely lacking the intuitive instinct of Detective Holmes, "I wonder why *I* don't have a uniform?" I mustered the courage to approach the austere Coach, stoically staring straight ahead through his silver and black, brow line glasses. "Hey Coach, when am I gonna get *my* uniform?" Seemingly oblivious to my question, he didn't even look at me, much less give me a reply. "Hey Coach, when am I gonna get *my* uniform?" I asked again, almost pleading. The third time's a charm, and I finally got a response, "Son, I don't know that you've even made the team," said Coach, with an air of steely finality. One thing he *did* know was that I had *not* made the team. I do *not* like baseball.

Meanwhile, back at the farm, in the middle to late 1970's, my parents were very tense people. They were good, God-fearing, church-going, hard-working, tax-paying, salt-of-the-earth kind of people, but tense. More times than I can remember, I'd hear my mother say "I'm so nervous I could die!" Her word for angst or anxiety was "uneasy." I heard her use that term a lot. It is actually a great and accurate term for anxiety, literally meaning, "not at ease." On occasion, I'd be riding down the road with her in our family car. She'd be behind the wheel, fussing up a storm in whispered bursts...to *herself*! Numerous times, someone was being royally chewed out! I'd ask her about it, and she would brush it aside. Funny thing is that I sometimes do the same thing. Touché!

In those years, daddy often seemed kind of stern and angry—not violent or physically abusive to me, just angry. Some of the tension was due to the fact that my parents and Donna were like oil and water, or maybe more accurately, the Santa Anna Winds and wildfire. She was the undisputed rebel of the family. Part of the tension, I suppose, was that those were just uptight times for conservative traditionalists like my parents.

At the behest of good friends, and after many years of hesitation, my mother enrolled at what was then Mayland Technical Institute (now Mayland Community College), and became a ward secretary at Cannon Memorial Hospital in

Banner Elk. The *M-A-Y* in Mayland stands for Mitchell, Avery, and Yancey counties, thus the name. Mayland has been such a Godsend to that area. In a few more years, mommy would become an RN, and an exceptional one at that, with the professional and personal accolades to prove it.

Here's the best part, the part that I've shared with many of my community college students over the past twenty years, especially my older female students. Hoping to inspire and motivate them, I share the fact that mommy was 47 years of age at the commencement of her final career journey, graduated at the top of her class, and worked in medical settings for about the next thirty years of her life. She was part of a generation that took few risks, especially if you happened to be female, and a mother at that.

Although she was underappreciated by her parents, in-laws, and some of her relatives, who placed little value on education or any attempt at self-betterment, she was undeterred. She might've appeared as a bundle of soft cotton, but that was merely a thin façade to cover a will and constitution of iron. She became the first person in her family to attend and graduate from college. She didn't merely break the mold, she broke it, ground it into powder, and scattered it to the Northwest wind.

I don't remember the exact dates, but Pam and Donna moved away in the early 70's. Larry finished his four-year stint in the Marine Corps, got married, and ended up in Illinois for several years, before eventually moving to Florida. Pam moved to the North Carolina coast, where she married, but after a divorce, eventually moved back to the area, and later remarried. Donna married in '78, and I in '82.

Much changed, and would continue to change fairly rapidly. I was making the transition from little boy to young man. Daddy was now working at Henredon Furniture in Spruce Pine, from which he would retire in 1984, and mommy had already undertaken her game-changing education and career journey.

Besides all the moves and transitions that had transpired, I lost my first grandparent in 1977, my paternal grandfather, Rob. In 1979, Great Grandfather, Rev. Garfield Hughes passed on. A steady stream of passings would soon follow in the coming years. Times, they were 'a changing. As is always true of life, it is a mixture of happy and sad, comings and goings, laughter and tears.

The effect that grandchildren have on their grandparents is amazing. Larry's two children, Donna's two, and my one, did much to level everyone out, and form tighter bonds in the family. Then, some of the grandchildren started having babies, and before you knew it, there were four generations of us.

Little by little, mommy wasn't nearly as "uneasy." Daddy became much more mellow, and amazingly and without explanation, gave up squirrel hunting (which he had dearly loved), groundhog hunting, and even trout fishing. He even started taking his pets to the veterinarian! Both parents became more openly affectionate with us, and had fewer reservations with saying "I love you."

If I live to be 119, I'll never forget my very last hug from daddy. It was 2004, his last Christmas. Less than a month later, he very literally dropped dead on January 22, 2005. Someone had given him a quart jar of strawberry-flavored moonshine, and his inhibitions were lowered just a wee bit, but in a good way. It was far and away the most heartfelt hug I ever received from him. God bless just a little 'alkihaul'! He squeezed my face so tightly against his that I could feel his beard stubble. He smelled of old-school aftershave, and just that inexpressible, flannel shirt-clad, manly man scent. Last things, final words, and timeless moments should never be forgotten. Important words must not go unspoken; important expressions must not be suppressed.

My beautiful sister, Pam, the Avery High Homecoming Queen of 1971, tragically passed of a devastating brain aneurysm in 1989. One redeeming virtue was that she and Donna had buried rusty old hatchets some time before that. Pam and I were never very close, but had she lived, I'm certain that we would've grown closer.

Well before Pam's passing, Donna and my parents had let the water run under the bridge, and had become very close. At the time of their departure—daddy's in 2005, and mommy's in 2012—two parents could not have hoped for a more caring, attentive, harder-working, loving daughter than sister Donna. At a certain point, hokey and clichéd as it might sound, they really *did* live happily ever after. My two surviving siblings and I, with very few, if any, substantial regrets, were able to see our precious parents pass, becoming closer with each other in the process. If I were facing a major crisis, and had to pick five people to be on my team, two of the five would be Larry and Donna. I know they'd have my back.

What a bipolar entity is time! So very cruel on some levels, so very kind on others, both a wounder and a healer, both an enemy and a friend. He takes us away, and brings us back, separates us, and binds us together.

In my life, particularly in my current vocation as a hospice chaplain, I've watched death make many rounds. Whether during an actual passing, or whether imminent, I see death up close and personal every single work day, and some others besides. I've concluded that the Grim Reaper almost always tends to do one of two things to families: he either rips them apart, or binds them together. With respect to my family, I'm eternally grateful that it was the latter. And in Death's defense, it's not actually *he* who rips or binds, it's merely *our* response to his never-ending role of separating us from this life, and leading us by the hand to the next.

I've never been in the presence of a dying person who grieved over not having had more money, who regretted not spending more time at the office or jobsite, or who wished that they had lived in a nicer house or driven a nicer car. Nor have I ever seen a moving van following a hearse. Not once have I personally witnessed any of these.

What I *have* witnessed is that at the end of the day, speaking quite literally, the only thing that really matters is the relationships that we have forged upon the anvil of life. These relationships have been made malleable by the fires of both passion and adversity. To be sure, upon that anvil, there are sparks flying every which way; blistering heat; grime; sweat; and the deafening clanging of relentless toil. But for better or for worse, in good times and bad, for beauty and ugliness, unbreakable links are formed. No two finished products are identical. I have begun to understand why blood truly is thicker than water.

Chapter 6: The Daze of My Life

In my parent's generation, education was something of a two-edged sword. It was not prioritized, but it was wrongly deemed the equivalent of intelligence. Daddy went only to the sixth grade. I think that's one of the reasons he felt inferior, or at least seemed to feel that way. However, he, and just about all of my close relatives, are very smart and immensely talented.

My grandparents and my parents both went to a one-room school, at the intersection of Jerry's Creek and Roaring Creek Road. I don't know the exact dates of their attendance, or to what grades they attended. My mother, and three of her five siblings, eventually ended up graduating from Cranberry High School in nearby Cranberry. In the 1940's-1960's, finishing high school in that area was quite an accomplishment.

Uncle Clyde attended school very little. He eventually dropped out completely in elementary school, even though the education of children had been mandatory in North Carolina since 1913. The reason he didn't attend was, well, because he didn't want to, and his parents didn't contest his wants. A highly skilled heavy equipment operator, he was very smart, but had no formal education.

From 1967-1975, I attended Minneapolis Elementary School. Considering my initial angst at having to hop on the big yellow school bus, number 34, and leave my comfort zone, I did fairly well at Minneapolis, and made the social adjustment just fine, almost as much as if I had been normal. It definitely did help me a lot, at the ripe old age of six, to discover girls!

In the 1960's and 70's, there was no such animal in our county as Junior High, and Minneapolis consisted of grades 1-8. I made so-so grades—a few A's, a few more B's, and several C's, but nothing lower than a C. My teachers were very strict, and some were so chronologically advanced that they had taught my father decades earlier. I was certain that some rode brooms to work, but decided not to make an inquiry. I'm being silly, of course, because all of my teachers were genuinely good people.

A few of the female teachers wore those pointy-rimmed glasses with blingy things that made them look a little bit like the rear fenders on a '57 Chevrolet. A word of unsolicited advice: never, *ever* test the limits of a lady wearing glasses donned with blingy things that make them look like the rear fenders on a '57 Chevy. I did twice: my first time and my last time. Lesson learned. Enough said.

Both during the elementary years, up until the present, I gravitated toward the language arts. Really, that seemed to be the emphasis at Minneapolis. It may not actually have been the case, but it seems that at Minneapolis, science and mathematics took a back seat to the language arts. Maybe that's just my bias talking. When I was in fifth grade, I was among a chosen few— about five or six of us I think—who got to do some classes with the sixth grade. Whoo hoo! my first and only stint as an advanced placement student.

At Minneapolis, I learned that I was a decent athlete, not Division I scholarship material, but decent. I could run and chew gum at the same time on the softball field, not trip over the half-court line in basketball, and was able to burst through any red rover wall of arms. I played seventh and eighth grade basketball. In eighth grade, I was the star player. I led my Wildcat team to a perfect record—0 wins 12 losses—perfect. Perfectly abysmal. I decided to retire from organized team sports after that.

One of the most significant investments my mother ever made was to buy a set of 1964 *World Book Encyclopedias*. I think she bought them mainly for me, and I was thrilled with the investment. Each year afterwards, you could get a one-volume update of new information for the previous year. For sentimental reasons, I kept that set for many decades, before reluctantly giving them up. Devouring those articles and pictures, I actually gave myself a pretty decent education. That's partly why to this very day, I am a veritable treasure trove of mostly useless, dated information. It does, however, on occasion, come in pretty handy as an armchair contestant on *Jeopardy*.

After Minneapolis came the big school, Avery County High School in Newland, the highest county seat east of the Mississippi River. I was mortified. With well under 1000 students (I think it was somewhere around 600 to 700), it wasn't even a large high school, but it was massively overwhelmingly to me. Having been ripped right out of the womb of my comfort zone at little Minneapolis Elementary, I was most definitely *not* socially well adjusted.

Angst was my constant companion at Avery. Added to that, Algebra I, for which I was woefully unprepared, swallowed me alive. Had it not been for an incredibly kind and patient algebra teacher, I would've received an F in Algebra I, but I passed with a 70T. 70 was a passing grade. In those days, a grade of 70T meant that you really *did not* pass, but you tried. Thank God for mercy, social promotion, and the letter T. I really did try.

Beyond the academic realm, Avery High was like a vast, barren desert of unfamiliar, unwelcoming faces. Some of that was my own fault of course. I had no initiative to resume any kind of organized sports, and perhaps worst of all, I had no peer group. I wasn't a jock, a nerd, a popular cool person, a club member, a rowdy bad boy type, an artsy type, or a redneck. I was more like an inconspicuous spot of mildew on the gymnasium walls. Uncomfortable in my own skin, I just simply didn't fit in, and didn't want to fit in. I merely wanted to survive and get out of Dodge. I wanted to quit in tenth grade (that was legal then), but my mother was very persuasive, and I toughed it out.

My one spark of hope and inspiration at Avery High was that, true to form, I had a modicum of interest in the language arts. In retrospect, I had some terrific teachers. I loved studying literature beneath the surface, and participating in class discussions. Not that it ever helped me land a job, but I can still recite most of the prologue to Chaucer's *Canterbury Tales.*

The years at Avery High finally died a slow, agonizing, but merciful death. Unconsciously, my favorite Scriptural expression in those four years was *"...and it came to pass...."*

What irony that after nine and a half additional years of education beyond high school, of both undergraduate and graduate studies, and twenty-one years after graduating high school, I found that my niche was teaching at the college level.

I had finally realized two traits about myself: (1) I really was a good student, capable of much more than C's and 70T's; (2) I loved to learn. It just took me a while driving the scenic route to figure that out. I always knew that I was smart enough to make passing grades without studying, but it took a while for me to find the focus button for the bigger picture.

Some of my past adjunct assignments as a college instructor have included teaching college courses for advanced placement high school seniors. One lesson I did learn, from my own experience as a high school student and much later as a teacher, is *never* to say to my students, "Students, these high school years are the best years of your life!" They were probably the worst consecutive four years for me personally. Some of my AP students, like me, didn't feel the warm fuzzies of high school either. So, I learned never to say that to my high school students. For many young people, just starting to learn how to navigate life, high school feels awkward or even perilous at times.

In 2009, I attended my thirtieth high school reunion, and found it to be somewhat twistedly comical and even validating. With a lot more confidence, and a lot less anxiety, and no pretenses of subtlety, I politely and practically forced some of the once-upon-a-time "cool people" to shake my hand and speak to me as one would expect mature adults to do. The comical part was the look of surprise on their faces that I had the audacity to force them to acknowledge me as an equal, and the fact that most of them continued to huddle together in the same little tribes of which they were a part at Avery High. At least I was able to disrupt the huddles, even if only for a few fleeting moments. It was so validating. I tried to engage everyone at that reunion—the pretty people, the not-so-pretty people, the cool people, the nerdy people, the good old boys—and with my beautiful wife at my side, I actually had a pretty good time.

I have heard, that in some people's case, high school defined them. If that were true for me, then my definition would be something like, "A nebulous cluster of anxious disconnect." I absolutely do not think that high school defined me. Thanks be to God! I prefer to believe, and have reason to believe that my definition took longer than that to write, and is still being written. I'll let you know if it's ever finished.

Chapter 7: And That's The Way We Were

By nature, Creekers and the Southern Appalachian Highlanders in general, are generally distrustful of government entities. I think that this is due in part to our fiercely independent Scot-Irish heritage.

In my single-digit years, the federal government considered us ("us" including my own immediate family) to be poor. They still classify many as such. I often heard of the poor, underprivileged people of Appalachia and felt sorry for them, but didn't realize we were some of the very ones being referenced.

Without a doubt, my parents and grandparents could've gotten some government subsidies, but other than commodity cheese, and silver cans with black lettering containing non-descript, generic *Peanut Butter* and *Pork,* they were far too proud to accept anything even approximating a handout. Then, to add insult to insult, the bureaucrat pointy-heads couldn't even pronounce *Appalachia!* They'd pronounce the second *a* as long *a.* I never knew we were poor, and wouldn't have cared even if I had known. I felt as rich as the legendary King Croesus.

What made creek life unique? Even among Avery County's small population of just over 17,000 residents, we were, and I suppose still are, regarded as *different.* Maybe that's justified. I suppose we are at least a little bit different. Well, maybe a whole lot different.

To begin with, we were/are referred to as *Creekers.* We who are such know that the term is not used simply to designate our geographical status. We were called *Creekers* by non-Roaring Creek residents mostly as a derisive and condescending label.

To be called a *Creeker* is to be classified as one of "them," i.e., different from "us."

On occasion, I used to hear folks say "Goooooshh! I heard that Roaring Creek is the meanest place in the country!" In all fairness, way back around the turn of the Twentieth Century, my Great Grandfather said that some of the Saturday night local good ol' boys would get liquored up and, in his words, "...went to frolics, which gave Roaring Creek a bad name which it rightly deserved...."

During his two years as Justice of the Peace, then six years as deputy sheriff, Grandpa 'Field helped bring law and order to the Valley. Not long ago I was visiting with a lady in her nineties, who was originally from a neighboring community in the vicinity of Roaring Creek. She originally hailed from Roan Mountain, Tennessee, literally, just a ridge over the state line. When I told her where I was from, she said, "Oh that's an awful place!" Old reputations die hard! It was such "an awful place" that my parents never locked our house, and they left their car keys in the ignition switch.

Some considered us Creekers to be on a lower rung on the social ladder. At least that was the distinct impression that was sometimes conveyed. That's fine with me, because I've always needed a bit of negative motivation to inspire that *I'll-show-you* edge. I like my Scot-Irish attitude!

Creekers were, and to a large degree still are, people who stay put. In my growing-up years, I never moved from the same house where my parents lived, beginning in 1955. I could say the same for scores of other families up there. Creekers don't mind occasionally visiting other parts of the country, but most of us just want to get home. Grandma Hazel was privileged to see several parts of the country, some of which I haven't. Grandma Nell, on the other hand saw very little.

Creekers are homebodies. I can remember vividly, even as a child, going no farther than Elizabethton, Tennessee; Johnson City, Tennessee; or Marion, Morganton, or Valdese, North Carolina, and then longing to get back home. I didn't like those places, and I really disliked the water. There's an old Creeker adage that goes: "If ever you drink the water on Roaring Creek, someday you'll come back." I couldn't imagine back then that *not* coming back would even be an option.

Creekers are true Stoics. The ancient Romans would've loved that. With their characteristic steely resignation, a combination no doubt of genetics and environment, Creekers just square their jaws, set their gaze, and let the bitter winds pelt them with come what may. "What will be will be," I heard often.

On numerous occasions, I heard daddy reference this or that man as, "a good solid fellar." That meant that whomever that 'fellar' happened to be, he was quiet, solemn, and consistently no-nonsense. For some reason, daddy really admired that demeanor. He himself had way too much of a sense of humor and love of telling a good story to fit his own description. Still, he most definitely *was* a "good, solid fellar," just not by his own definition.

In my immediate family and in my mother's immediate family, it was not acceptable physically to show or verbally express affection. In fact, my mother looked disapprovingly on that. She deemed it superficial and unnecessary. In retrospect, I think that was a defense mechanism that arose out of her own hurt and disappointment. "I/we love you" was something that was to be silently understood, but not verbally or physically acknowledged. I instinctively knew that was off somehow, and vowed to myself that my life would be lived differently. It was deemed appropriate to express anger, but not overt joy or love.

My father's side of the family was very affectionate, both physically and verbally. There's a truckload of psychology to be unloaded in all that by someone more qualified than I. A good psychiatrist would've had a heyday among my folks. Thankfully, that part of my family did greatly improve.

As an extension of their Stoic tendency, Creekers tend toward melancholy. It seems that all "signs" observed by Creekers are portents of doom. Almost nothing ever predicted good. For example, when a circle appears around the moon, you count the number of stars inside the circle to determine how many days of *bad weather* would follow. Grandpa Jack had a way of predicting the number of snows in the winter: it was determined by the number of times there was fog on Big Yellow Mountain in August. Some years, he was pretty darned close.

Superstition was, and I suppose still is to a certain degree, ingrained in the very fabric of folks on the Creek. I can remember that on a few occasions, Grandma Hazel would visit a lady down on Powdermill Road, about three miles away, to "...have some warts talked off." Maybe I should find someone to "...talk some hair back on."

My mother claimed not to be superstitious, but she would insist on black-eyed peas, hog jowls, greens, cabbage, and a few other dishes to be served on New Year's Day. She didn't even like black-eyed peas. That meal must have had the reverse effect, because it seems that nearly every January, hell itself would be unleashed, usually in the form of flood.

Old-time Creekers, my parents included, religiously abided by the signs of the moon. With regard to everything from when the crops were planted, when the crops were harvested, when the crops were canned, and even when fence posts were driven into the black earth, the signs had to be taken into account.

Mommy was adamant that crops and such had to be planted and preserved under the right signs, and that certain tasks were to be done only under the right sign. For example, according to her, if you pickled corn or made sauerkraut when the signs were in the bowels, the results would be utterly awful. I grew a little bit of corn in Tennessee one year, and when it came time to harvest it, I did so, and took it to my mother to ask her to pickle it for me. She had a conniption fit! The signs weren't right, she said, and it won't be fit to eat! I pleaded with her do it anyway, since freshly pulled, shucked corn can't be put on hold. It was as delicious as ever.

Chalk it up to the hard farm life there in the mountains, combined with poor economic conditions, and maybe the long winters, but for whatever reasons, Creekers are not a real cheery, positive bunch. They have the uncanny ability always to see a dark cloud behind a silver lining. If I've heard it once, I've heard it eight hundred times after a person in the community passed away, "Well, it's somn' coming to all of us!" How comforting.

I don't have any scientific statistics at hand, but I would wager that there is a higher-than-normal rate of depression there in the mountains. I do know that Avery County has a high per capita suicide rate in the state of North Carolina. It makes me sad to ponder how differently some people's lives would have/could have been with the excellent treatments now available for various mental illnesses. I absolutely believe that there are millions who should/could still be living who have died, and whose lives could have been so much better.

Basic simplicity is another trait Roaring Creekers cherish. Some of those old land deeds reflected this for better or worse, and truthfully, sometimes it was for worse. "Robert Hughes's property line runs up the hill to the big white oak stump, and then...." Legal transactions used to be sealed with verbal agreements and firm handshakes. That's admirable, but trouble is, given enough time, stumps eventually rot and disappear, and some people don't keep their agreements!

Socio-economically, Creekers range from poverty-level, working poor, to middle-class. Most would probably fall into the lower-middle-class bracket. Other than crop farming, which has now been surpassed by Fraser Fir farming, Roaring Creek has never had any real industry to speak of.

It seems that nearly all of the adult men, at least in my parents' generation, could do just about anything that required mechanical or constructive skill. Some were first-rate carpenters, some could do plumbing, electrical work, masonry, etc. They *had* to do those things. When something had to be done, you didn't pick up the phone and call Mr. Handy Dandy, you just did it. I'm pretty sure that the mechanical/constructive gene skipped me. Every time I botch some sort of project, I can still hear my father's voice as clearly as the Tarheel Mica Company quittin' time whistle, "Chris, honey, I swear to goodness! You could tear up a' anvil with a rubber hammer!" I can't help it if my gifts aren't primarily *constructive*. My, what a career I could have had as a demolitionist!

There has always been a considerable degree of musical and artistic talent on the Creek. Quite a number of folks are adept at playing stringed instruments and vocal performance. The Hopson's are especially gifted in the music department.

Some of our folks formed gospel, country, and bluegrass groups, performing in churches and/or private homes. Every one of those branches and hollers holds unheralded gems of musical talent. Oddly enough, no one in my immediate family sang or played an instrument except for me. On my mother's side, there were a number of singers and musicians.

Two of the highest degrees of talent hailing from the Creek, in my opinion, are storytelling and writing. Among others, brothers Grady and Lloyd Hughes were phenomenal storytellers. I think either, particularly Grady, could have blown away the audiences at the Jonesborough International Storytelling festival, only twenty miles or so from my current home.

In terms of writing, I earlier mentioned Ms. Zora Greene. She had that *X Factor* quality about her writing that just ushered you back across the seas of time, on a magic carpet of nostalgia. And of course, there was, and still is, Bertie Burleson. Bertie, a family friend, was a long-time fixture at the Avery Journal and later the Avery Post. She wrote various types of articles, wrote of the comical exploits of "Aunt Keziah," and still writes soulful pieces of poetry and short stories. I love her writing.

For those who weren't self-employed, it was not at all uncommon, and still isn't to the very present, to drive twenty, thirty, or even sixty miles one way to find work. In the 1930's and 40's, a number of Creek families moved north, particularly Canton, Ohio, to find work in the factories, humming with production in the post-WWII era. Uncle Max, who lived up Jerry's Creek, married one of mommy's sisters, Aunt Wanda. They ended up in Canton. Uncle Max was a super guy who was a ton of fun to be around, and passed much too soon.

A lot of the men from the Creek worked in timber and sawmilling in foreign countries like Maryland or Virginia. Some married girls from "up North." Several of them returned home, some didn't. I guess Creek life isn't for everyone.

In kinder, gentler times, most of the mom-and-pop country stores allowed store credit. The proprietors knew whom they could trust. Grandpa Jack had a running tab with both R.S. Burleson and Erwin's Grocery.

Up until sometime in the 1970's, the two little grocery stores had a very tasty incentive for customers like Grandpa Jack, who always paid their store credit bill in a timely manner. It was an old-timey version of a credit card cash-back program.

Upon full payment of his store credit, Grandpa Jack would bring home what we fondly referred to as "the big poke." To show their appreciation for their customers' business, the proprietors would fill up a good-sized paper poke full of good candy—Hershey's bars, Butterfingers, Reese's Cups, Milky Ways, and the like.

One particular time, I remember Grandpa Jack getting the "big poke" at R.S. Burleson's. Barely had we left the parking lot in that tired, old, teal Chevrolet truck, until I dove into that bag of candy like a gold prospector. "Yum! A moist, cellophane-wrapped brownie!" thought I. I ripped off the clear cellophane, and took a big bite of what turned out to be plug tobacco! It wasn't that I was above taking a jaw-full of tobacco, even plug style, but trust me when I tell you that when you're expecting to sink your teeth into a brownie, and it turns out to be plug tobacco, it's an experience not soon forgotten.

Further south, in the Ingalls community, about ten miles from Roaring Creek, we had Joe Howell's Store. If you couldn't find it at Joe Howell's, then you probably didn't need it to begin with. Joe's store was like a much smaller version of one of the big home improvement stores, but way more fun and unique. Eventually, Joe added a grocery side to his store. Then he was really big time!

Joe Howell's was by no means the least expensive place to shop, but daddy did business with him anyway. The reason was because daddy, and I guess just about everybody else, loved Joe Howell. Besides that, daddy was loyal. He knew he would pay more at Joe's, but he didn't care.

You could buy things "on time" as they called it, well before very many people had credit cards. I too loved Joe, and followed in daddy's footsteps, buying a couple of guns from him back in the early 80's. I was going to buy a third, but I had met the girl of my dreams, my future wife. I backed out of the "on-time" deal, and Joe jokingly but prophetically asked "What did you do, decide to get married instead?" Actually, that was exactly what I had decided to do, and knew I'd better put my material wants on hold.

Demographically, Roaring Creek is virtually 100% white. That was true when I grew up there, and is still largely true today. Avery County is one of the largest producers of shrubbery in the U.S., particularly Christmas trees. Over the past thirty-plus years or so, there has been a fairly significant influx of Hispanic migrant workers, who earn their bread by the sweat of their brow in the fields of fragrant evergreens.

Roaring Creek was, and to only a slightly lesser degree now, perfectly happy and fiercely guarded with its isolation. Anyone with even a slight northern or other accent was deemed a "Yankee," or at the least "not from around here." I have a separate chapter on language, accent, etc. Creekers were highly suspicious, mistrusting, and guarded with respect to outsiders. Yet, "outsiders" were politely tolerated.

Before desegregation, there was one school in Avery County for black children, located between the Powdermill and Crab Orchard communities, along the banks of Toe River. I regret that I don't remember the name of that school, nor has anyone been able to tell me.

After desegregation, at the very head of the main branch of Roaring Creek, there lived our only black residents in the entire community. I don't remember if the father was a sharecropper or what, I'm thinking he was, but they lived in the old Joe Stihl place.

Joe, an "outsider" from somewhere in Virginia, lived at the very head of the main Roaring Creek Road in a newer house. I believe that it was our loss that we didn't get to know him better. My brother, Larry, did get to know him, and really liked him, having taken flying lessons from him.

At any rate, this black family was at the old Stihl place for what seemed like a very short duration. I also remember that from this family, one small girl, younger, and a few grades behind me, rode my school bus, old number 34.

At that time, ironically enough, my bus, and the high school bus were both driven by two incredible black gentlemen, brothers Ed and Reuben Jackson, from Beech Bottom, a community about two miles from Roaring Creek. There were just a handful of black neighbors who lived in Beech Bottom and nearby Licklog.

During the school year, Ed would stop at my Uncle Herman's store every morning and every afternoon on his bus route, and have a cold Dr. Pepper in a glass bottle. I'll never drink another Dr. Pepper without remembering Ed Jackson. Another irony is that one of my very best school buddies was Johnny Mathes, a black guy who also hailed from the Beech Bottom community.

To my shame, I don't even know what that little aforementioned black girl's name was. She was slender, immaculately groomed, well dressed, and sat in her bus seat straight as an arrow and silent as a tomb. Much to my embarrassment, I don't recall ever having spoken a word to my little sister of color.

Now, goaded by the barbs of time, regret, and memory, I can only imagine, and that very poorly, how that little girl must have felt in that strange, unfamiliar, all-white world of strange-talking people. For all practical purposes, she was essentially invisible, unheard, insignificant. She was, in that community at least, little more than a desegregation statistic. What was her name? I don't know. What were her parents' names? I don't know. Where did she come from? I don't know. How many siblings did she have; what did she do for fun; what were her favorite subjects in school; what kind of work did her daddy do; where did she go to church; did she like it here? I don't know.

Just before I left home for the very first time, heading off to Bible college in Greenville, South Carolina, my Uncle Jerry Guinn and I were having a conversation at his home. Jerry is my Aunt Sandra's (on my mother's side) husband. Uncle Jerry said something to me that he may possibly have forgotten, but which I have never forgotten. He looked me dead in the eye and said with utter earnestness "Don't *ever* look down on anyone." He spoke from personal experience. I think he told me this because one, he knew what it felt like to be on the receiving end of condescension; and two, I was getting ready to go away to Bible college, and that sort of thing can inflate some people's ego. During those three years in Greenville, I don't think my ego was inflated, only the homesickness in my heart. I just wanted to finish up and go back home, but the admonition stuck.

To varying degrees, we are all composite products of our DNA, our environment, our culture, and our experiences, both good and bad—i.e., nature *and* nurture. Statistics and demographics are much easier to deal with than people. Statistics and demographics are devoid of emotions, interactions, hopes, and dreams. They're not intimate, don't communicate, or touch your soul. They're just numbers.

That little nameless African princess; that dirt-poor white girl with a foul odor, living in no telling what kind of hellish home; dozens of other scruffy ragamuffins who smelled of wood smoke, sweat, and meat grease, and wore dirty clothes and tattered shoes—they were no mere statistics. Either by ancestry, or merely by the fact that they were in my cultural sphere, they were and still are part of my own story.

Unwittingly, they taught me some of the values, that to this day, I fiercely embrace, and try to embody. Sometimes I get it right, sometimes I don't. Sometimes I can see through the invisibility, sometimes not. Sometimes I can hear beyond the silence, sometimes not. Those unheard, unheralded, unremarkable little teachers—regardless of race, upbringing, or socio-economic category—unwittingly taught me to champion the underdog; speak for those who have no voice; at least be a presence for those who have no one; take the initiative for those too inhibited and too downtrodden to lead, but too important to be ignored; and never, *ever*, under any circumstance look down on anyone.

The way we *were* has neither the power nor the authority to dictate who we *are*. Ever learning, we never graduate during this life. Ever seeking, we never fully discover everything in this life. Ever traveling, we never arrive in this life. Unceasingly, steadily, deliberately, we *become.*

Chapter 8: That Roaring Creek Brogue

Of all possible times and places to have had a cultural/ancestral epiphany, this was surely one of the oddest and least expected. It was on or about June 9, 2009. I was entering my second of a two-week pilgrimage to Israel with twenty-two other Christian ministers from various denominations and parts of the U.S. It was one of those once-in-a-lifetime opportunities, for which I am profoundly grateful.

The first week of the pilgrimage had been spent in the northern part of the country, in and around Tiberias. During the second week, we stayed at ground zero, epicenter of the world, the holy city itself—Jerusalem. That second week was spent at Jerusalem's magnificent Pontifical Institute, the Notre Dame Jerusalem center. The Notre Dame features a towering French cathedral and guest house. We stayed in the guest house, not at all lavish, but inviting, spacious, clean, and well kept. The Notre Dame is located in modern Jerusalem, directly across the street from the New Gate, one of the portals entering the walled city, Old Jerusalem.

Shortly before our first evening's dinner, Father Kelly, an energetic, congenial Irish Catholic priest who served as our host, took our eager group to the rooftop of the one of the Notre Dame's buildings for a visual tour. From that lofty perch, we were treated to an awe-inspiring panoramic view of the old city. It felt surreal to be standing there. I could scarcely believe that a boy from Roaring Creek was standing in that spot at that moment, staring at one of the most important places on earth.

Father Kelly gave us a quick but enormously helpful debriefing of the various sections of Old Jerusalem, particularly as they related to Jesus' trial and Passion. Without a single written note, or map, or a moment's hesitation, Father Kelly directed our attention to this spot, that spot, this direction, and that, all of which related to the places and people connected to the final days and hours of Jesus' Passion. He could have done it in his sleep.

Pointing to our right, he said in his heavy Irish accent, "Over there, to the South, was the house of Caiaphas. And then Jesus was taken there…then He was taken there…and then…" (fasten your seatbelt—the moment is imminent), "He was taken *Narth* to the Antonia Fortress and appeared before Pilate.…" So help me God, as I stood on a high roof overlooking the Holy City itself, that Irish priest said *Narth*. That was it. You were expecting an earth-shaking revelation, weren't you? Insignificant as it may seem, the pronunciation of that one, single-syllable word, *Narth,* was momentous for me.

I can't remember anything else Father Kelly said during that visual tour after he said *Narth*. A deep chord had been struck. Roots were unearthed. I was suddenly awash with a cascade of ancestral awareness. Hazy images whisked through my mind of early Scot-Irish settlers, finding and winding their way into the Southern Appalachians, no doubt feeling right at home.

That Irish priest unknowingly became a living window, and legitimate link to my past. I feel really dense for it to have taken me so long to realize it, but it suddenly made a lot more sense why my people spoke in our peculiar accent, pronouncing *North* as *Narth,* as but only one example.

Some things are like terrible car wrecks—you hate to look, but you just can't turn away. That's how I am when it comes to the pronunciation of our splendid words, *Appalachian* and *Appalachia.* I can't begin to tell you how appreciative I am of the fact that you're reading my book, but if we are to stay on good terms, then we have to come to an understanding. That third *a* in *Appalachian* or *Appalachia* is pronounced as the *a* in *latch.* Phonetically, the two words are *Ap-uh-latch'-un/Ap-uh-*

latch' -uh respectively. Just repeat those words three times and you'll have it. On the other hand, if you are obstinate in the acquisition and processing of new information, and come up on Roaring Creek and start that long *a*, *Appalāchian* mess, don't blame me if you receive a less- than-warm welcome.

Hardly anything grates on my nerves to a greater degree than hearing a poorly executed, fake Southern accent in a movie or TV show. The would-be Southern-talkers sound as if they're trying to eat a mouthful of parsnips after having a Novocain injection. Rarely do the actors and directors get it right. That being said, there's a nerve-wracking fallacy I need to clear up before I blow a gasket.

A Southern Appalachian accent is as distinct from a Deep South accent, or a Carolina Piedmont accent, or a Virginia Tidewater accent, as a Brooklyn accent is from a northern Minnesotan accent. Everyone whose accent is different from their own refers to the other as "having an accent." We *all* have accents, sweet pea, it's just a matter of *which one* we have.

You may have noticed already, but the Deep South accent often has an aversion to the letter *R*. Butter is *butta*. Letter is *letta*, etc. Conversely, the Southern Appalachian accent *loves* the letter *R*. I haven't conducted a poll or done a linguistic investigation, but I'm pretty sure that *R* is our favorite consonant.

There's not a tremendous amount that I've said thus far that differentiates the Creekers from most native Avery Countians, or for that matter, the greater Southern Appalachian region. I'd bet the farm, however, that if I were to ask local, native Avery Countians what sets Roaring Creek apart, the resounding answer would be *the dialect,* or as some would say with a bit of a smirk, "…that old Roaring Creek brogue!"

On too many occasions to recall, I vividly remember the frequent response that total strangers, native Avery Countians at that, would exhibit upon learning that yours truly was from Roaring Creek. It would usually be accompanied by a condescending remark, pathetically attempting to duplicate the distinct Roaring Creek dialect. I'd hear, *"Rarring Crack!"* or *"Rarring Crick!"* or some such nonsense. One more car wreck: I can't let pass the fact that the pronunciation of *creek* as *crick* is normally not even Southern Appalachian. It may have a hillbilly-sounding twang, but it's actually used more in other parts of the country like the Midwest or Northeast, e.g. You're welcome.

Among linguistic scholars, some have said that the peculiar Southern Appalachian Highlands' dialect is the original one spoken in the American colonies. Some say that particular dialect can be traced all the way back to the Old English period (c. 5th—11th Centuries CE), even to towering figures such as Chaucer. Such bold declarative statements are the fodder of verbal altercations amongst the linguistic scholars and historians, neither of which I am. We can at least agree that it does indeed have its own peculiar sound.

Admittedly, the distinctive dialect of Roaring Creek is very difficult, if not impossible in some cases, to duplicate in writing. I'll give it my best shot without any guarantees. I've garnered some common Roaring Creek words and expressions, the great majority of which are commonly used in other parts of the Southern Appalachians. The list does not include some of the usual Southern Appalachian words (*taters* and *maters*, e.g.) that are as common as cornbread and catfish throughout the South. There are only a few of the words and expressions that I've listed (marked with an asterisk*) that I personally have *not* heard outside of Roaring Creek, but some of which are said to be spoken in other parts of the South. What follows is a partial list.

Agin—Against

Aig [*Ai* pronounced as *aye*]—Egg

Airy/Airyn'—A single one

Alkihaul [*ki* as in *key*]—Alcohol

Ar—Arrow

Arish—Irish

Arn—Iron

Arnge—Orange

Art—Ought, should

Artn't—Ought not, should not

Aught—The number 0 [Aught can mean: "anything at all." E.g. "Do you know aught?" I heard only the first usage, i.e., 0.]

Awf'lst—Most awful; E.g. "That was the awf'lst racket I ever hyerd!"

Banjer—Banjo

Bile—Boil

*Brile—Broil, e.g., "Ive been out in that hot brilin' sun!"

Bryar(s) [*yar* as in yard]—Briar(s)

*Bum—Bomb

*B'yer [Single syllable; *er* as in *her*]—Beer

*B'yerd [Single syllable; *er* as in *her*]—Beard

Carn—Corn

Cher [*er* as in *her*]—Chair

*Cicero—0° Fahrenheit, e.g., "Hit got down to cicero last night!"

Clim—Past tense of climb

*Come in one hair—Almost; E.g. "He come in one hair of runnin' off the road!"

*C'yarn— Cairn; carrion, i.e., rotten flesh

D'mater—Tomato

Dannimite—Dynamite

*Drap—Drop

D'rectly—Shortly, momentarily e.g., "I'll be thar d'rectly."

Eech—Itch (Eech can be used as either a noun or a verb. E.g., "I've got a' eech on my lag. I wanna eech it!")

Far—Fire; for

Fer/Fer Piece—Far/A long ways

*Fine'ly Teetote'ly—Completely; E.g. "He fine'ly teetote'ly rern't [ruined] his new shirt."

Fit—Fought

*Foolish-Headed—Feeling dizzy; not feeling quite right in the head

*Gaumed up mess—A complete mess that's been made of something. E.g., "That's the awf'lst gaumed up mess I've ever seen in my life!"

Git'ar—Guitar

Haint/Hainted—Ghost or spirit/Haunted

Hain't—Same as "ain't;" is not/are not

Her'n—3rd person possessive *hers*

His'n—3rd person possessive *his*

Hit/Hit's/Hits—It/It is/Its

*Hope—Help—can be either present tense "I need fer ye to hope me;" or past tense "If you hadn't a hope me, I would't a got done."

*Hyerd [*er* as in *her*]—Heard

If I had to die!—Exclamatory expression equivalent to, "That is unbelievable!"

*I'll swan!—Exclamatory expression such as "Oh my goodness!"

Lag—leg

Lard—Lord, as in "the good Lord"; lard, as in hardened animal fat.

Learn—In the mountain dialect, learn is often used for "teach." E.g., "Can you learn me how to play the git'ar?"

*Long-Headed—Wild or unruly in conduct e.g., "Look goin' at that long-headed thang!"

*Mess—A hearty portion of food, e.g. "I cooked a mess of backbones and ribs."

*Motisicle—Motorcycle

Narth—North

Nary/Naryn/Nary singl' one—Not one/Not a single one

*Neen—Need not, needn't

*O Thee—Touché!

*Pitch and Stave—To walk as if intoxicated or in an awkward manner

*Plime Blank—Exactly, precisely [Said to be used outside of Roaring Creek, but I have not personally heard it.]

*Pizen [long i]—Poison

Plum—completely

Plum Foolish—Completely crazy; ridiculous

Pone—Either a swollen area of the body, e.g. "My wrist is poned up"; or a cake of bread, e.g., "a *pone* of cornbread"

Pyert—[*er* as in *her*]—Pert; energetic

Quare—Queer as in strange or odd. "He acts sarter quare."

Raynch [*ay* as in aye]—A wrench; to wrench; rinse

Rern't—Ruined

Sarter—Sort of

*Sack Naz/The Old Sack Naz—Satan, or the devil [My maternal grandmother is the only person from

whom I ever heard this expression. I've no idea where it originated.]

Sodie Pop/A Dope—Soda pop

Sot—A severe alcoholic

Tar(s)—Tire(s)

Ther'n—3rd person possessive *theirs*

Tore up/Tore all t' pieces—Fairly common Southern Appalachian terms meaning broken, broken down, destroyed. E.g. "He wrecked his motisicle and tore hit all t' pieces."

War— Wire

Warry—Worry

Winder [Short *i* as in *win*]—Window

*Wisht'm'never—Exclamatory term expressing shock or surprise similar to "Oh my goodness!!"

Womern—Woman

Yaller—Yellow

*Yander—Same as yonder

Youn's—2nd person plural [Note: I don't recall *ever* hearing any of my people use the common Southern term, *"ya'll."*]

Your'n—2nd person singular possessive your/yours

Yourn'ses—2nd person plural possessive your/yours

*Yer(s) [*er* as in her]—ear(s)

I'm as certain as death and taxes that there are probably a bushel basket of words and expressions that I forgot to include, and some that I deliberately omitted because of the sheer volume. So, the preceding list is merely representative. I've been fascinated for some time with some other aspects of *that old Roaring Creek brogue* that reach beyond vocabulary and expressions. Let's look at those.

My Uncle Clyde (mother's side) used some of the oddest expressions that I've ever heard. It was decades before I realized that many of those expressions meant absolutely nothing, and were based on absolutely nothing. They just came from somewhere in his mind. For example, he'd say "That gentleman come one hair of goin' up the Joe Road!" *Joe Road* referred to nothing. It was just a Clydeism that meant "He almost died or encountered tragedy."

We once had a pastor at the Missionary Baptist church to whom Clyde referred as "Little Charlie." That wasn't the pastor's name, and the pastor, not a local, couldn't figure out to save his life, to whom Clyde was referring. He was referring to absolutely no one. It was just a name that popped into his head.

One more: "He's nearly ready for the green coat!" It was another Clydeism that was evocative of men in white lab clothes taking someone away to a psychiatric facility. Again, *green coat* corresponded to nothing that was literally true.

For reasons that are beyond my expertise, a lot of Creekers have a strong aversion to the schwa sound, i.e., vowels pronounced as "uh." For example, California is pronounced by some as Californie; Georgia is pronounced as Jargie; dynamite is pronounced dannimite.

What's really interesting is when we get into proper names with a schwa ending. I was nearly grown before I realized that some of my fellow Creekers had official given names far different from what I ever knew. Cousin Verna was always pronounced *Vernie*; cousin Coda was *Cody*; cousin Eva was *Evie*; Laura was either *Lar* or *Laurie*.

I've had some personal experience with the schwa prejudice. My wife's name is Tonia. The first time I introduced her to my maternal Grandmother Hazel, the latter said (with perfectly good pronunciation) "I can't say 'Tonia,' I'll just call you 'Connie.'" That's proof positive of schwa discrimination if ever there was any such proof!

A telling indicator of one's Creek background is the pronunciation of the diphthongs "ai" and "ou." Get your mind out of the gutter—a diphthong has nothing to do with lingerie or swimwear. A diphthong is a vowel combination that creates one sound when pronounced. Two examples: *haunted* and *our.* "Au" in *haunted,* and "ou" in *our* are both diphthongs.

I don't think that I am able adequately to express the distinctive "ai" and "ou" pronunciation in writing, but I'll give it a try. Here are few representative words. *Ayair* = Air—the stuff we breathe. You have to try and imagine someone pronouncing that word with their lower lip twisted to one side and pronouncing it almost like a pirate saying *Arrrgh. Haiyr* = hair. Then there's *ou. Auer* = (depending on context) *our* or *hour.* The "a" is short "a" as in "at." Both examples are pronounced as single syllable words. Sorry, I did my best, but you're on your own with the rest of it.

The Creek dialect dislikes the *or* sound—George, Orange, Horse, Gorge, North, etc. Again, my assumption is that this came across the Atlantic from the British Isles. If you listen closely to some citizens from the UK, you can hear this sound, particularly it seems, by those from Scotland or Ireland. *Or* gets replaced by *ar*. In my short list above—*Jarge* = George; *Arnge* = Orange; *Harse* = Horse; *Linville Garge* = Linville Gorge; *Narth* = North, etc.

Another linguistic peculiarity (and I'm probably forgetting some others of no small importance) is also beyond my power of explanation. Creekers use a lot of truncated or cut-off names. Tons of people throughout my life have asked me if my official name is *Christopher.* It is not, and that's just as well, because I would've been called Chris (or worse) anyway. It's not a respect or lack thereof issue, it's simply an idiom of the dialect.

Great Grandfather, Baptist preacher Garfield, was affectionately referred to by nearly everyone as *Gyar*, or *Preacher Gyarfield.* Paternal Grandfather Robert was *Rob*, and his wife, Grandmother Nellie, was *Nell*. Cousin Irene was simply *Reen*. Way back generations ago before my time, there was a Webb gentleman name Nebraska, but I always heard him referred to as *Brack,* and another named Sylvester, who was referred to as *Vester*.

Those with initial names such as J.G. and S.D. had it made. One of my best buddies from childhood was a leather-tough, sinewy little Young fellow from Martin's Branch, one of our hollers on Roaring Creek. His given name was Garrett Coyd Young, but no one knew him by any other name than simply *G.C.* I swear by the hair that used to be on my head that we, well, maybe I, found a way to shorten even *G.C.* Sometimes we simply called him *G.*

One of the peculiarities of *Creekese* is the manner of differentiation between *Senior* and *Junior*. It seems that in most cases if a male happened to be Junior (George, Jr. e.g.), he would likely be referred to simply as *Junior*. My parents' first child was George Jason, Jr., the one who died during birth. Had he lived, he more than likely would have been known as *Junior Hughes*.

There was one other manner of distinguishing Senior and Junior, and that was by use of the adjectives *Big* and *Little*. E.g., there once was a father/son tandem named Hamilton Hopson, Sr. and Hamilton Hopson, Jr., known to all of us simply as *Big Ham* and *Little Ham*. That may seem odd, but there was no confusion as to whom was being referenced.

Language and the ability to communicate distinguish us as human. Admittedly, geography and culture can often make our communication a challenge. I have a devil of a time understanding the good folks from the Northeast. To my slow-processing ears, combined with a hearing impairment, their accent, coupled with their rapid speech and sometimes-brusque manner, makes their communication sound like a roomful of guinea fowl pecking on electric typewriters. Just keeping it real here.

It was sometime in the mid-1970's that I, minding my own business on a warm summer day, found myself walking down the dusty gravel road about a quarter of a mile below my house. I don't remember where I was going, but just a few yards past the People's Church, right before the gravel road ended and the paved road began, a strange car approached. *Strange*, in this context, meaning *not recognizable as belonging to us*. It was a nice-looking car, a 70-something Ford LTD, light blue, dark blue vinyl roof, without a single scratch, dent, or rattle that I could detect. Everybody knew everybody else's car or truck. This clean, shiny, blue LTD stood out like a piano in a Church of Christ.

As the blue Ford approached, a bespectacled gentleman, who looked as clean and shiny as his alien craft, lowered his driver's window and clearly wanted to communicate. With words that sounded to my large ears like the clanking and crunching of an eleven-car pileup, he said in a very hurried tone "Pardonme, butcanyoutellmehowtogetto Crunbereé?"

There were a couple of other people in the car, but they didn't say anything. I'm no detective, but I clearly and quickly deducted that he *wasn't from around here*. "Sppiittt," said the tobacco juice launched from my lips, and I said, "Doo whaat?" Understand that a Creeker can turn two simple one-syllable words into at least four syllables. But this was my turf, and at least I didn't talk like I had a mouthful of bumblebees. He repeated his statement which, from the inflection of the words, I realized was a question. "Canyoutellmehowtogetto Crunbereé?" I was proud of my ability to follow a foreign language, at least partially, and did pretty well except for that last, strongly inflected word in his hurried question, *Crunbereé.* I really and truly did want to help Mr. Spick and Span and the befuddled passengers in his shiny light blue Ford, but *Crunbereé?* I was clueless. "Sppiittt. Noo, I ain't never hyerd of it."

He thanked me just the same and wheeled his LTD around in the parking lot of the People's Church to head back in the other direction. As he passed me, I saw that his car tag said *Ontario.* I definitely had the geographical part of this mystery man down pat—by golly, he really wasn't from around here! He was a *loooong* ways from here!

Like a bolt of lightning on top of Big Yellow Mountain, it struck me. Being a lad with keen powers of deduction, I finally figured out that *Crunbereé* had to be *Cranberry*, a little unincorporated community, about ten miles north or fifteen minutes' drive from where I had stood, talking unintelligibly to somebody in a nice blue LTD from Ontario.

I sincerely hope that my polite neighbor from north of the border found his way to *Crunbereé,* and that he eventually forgave that unhelpful twelve-year-old with the blank stare. And if I did inadvertently get any tobacco spit on that shiny light blue Ford, it was purely unintentional.

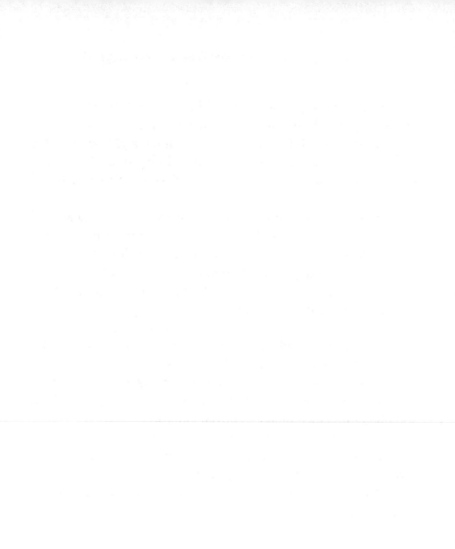

Chapter 9: Good Soup Beans Don't Rattle

If it oinked, mooed, or clucked; if it swam, climbed trees, or flew; chances are, we considered it edible. Great, Great Grandfather Wilson, better known as Brothe (pronounced as *Brother* minus the final *r*), said that an owl was the toughest thing he ever tried to eat. Lord have mercy! We raised our own pork, beef, chicken, and supplemented those protein sources with trout from the creek, squirrels from the woods, and groundhogs from the fields. We ate plenty, ate healthier than we realized, and we ate well.

Our diet consisted of much more than pork, beef, chicken, and wild game. We raised and preserved a lot of vegetables and fruits. Virtually every family on Roaring Creek grew Irish potatoes, several varieties of beans, and corn. Those were the big three. Besides those, my family grew cabbage, sweet peppers, leaf lettuce, onions, squash, cucumbers, English peas, beets, carrots, strawberries, black raspberries, and tomatoes. In the pre-electricity days, fruits and vegetables were canned mostly in quart and pint jars, and some in half gallons. The practice of canning continued even after all the homes had electricity. How I would love to have another jar of Grandma Nell's canned corn!

A lot of our vegetables were pickled, including beans, corn, cabbage, peppers, and beets. For nearly half of my life, I didn't realize that people ate beets in ways other than pickled. After trying stewed beets, I can understand why some don't like them. It's a crying shame that they couldn't have started out on pickled beets. Freshly processed beet juice, by the way, makes my top four list for *The Worst-Tasting Things I've Ever Put in My Mouth*, right behind black licorice candy, magnesium sulfate, and root beer.

Every year, around late August to early September, my mother pickled a five-gallon ceramic crock of corn on the cob. Half runner and blue lake green beans were pickled in quart jars. Pickled corn on the cob is one of those foods in which no middle ground exists. No one ever tries it and says "It's OK, I guess." Nope. It's either love or hate. To state it mildly, I love the stuff.

After the necessary amount of time (about a week and a half to two weeks, I think) in the big ceramic crock, which was safely stored in the cellar, the pickling salt and water worked their magic. It was time. I'd take the cotton pillow case off the top of the crock, push aside a thick layer of mold, and then remove a two-pound rock or maybe a quart jar of sauerkraut that held down a large glass dinner plate. The weighted plate's job was to keep the corn submerged in the pickling solution. Ah! Salty-tangy, yellow gold! I'd immerse my hand in the solution, retrieving the pickled ears. Sometimes I'd have five or six ears of it. The briny solution, along with some of the mold, would drip off my elbows, while I fared sumptuously on my favorite September treat. When your elbows were dripping, it tasted even better.

Some of the tree fruits that we preserved had to come mostly from sources other than our own. Other than apples, cherries, and plums, the mountains simply have too short of a growing season for some other fruits, like good peaches, for example. The few peaches that we did manage to grow weren't much bigger than ping pong balls. Peaches were usually purchased from local peddlers who had hauled them out of South Carolina. We canned them in quart jars, or froze them.

Blackberries grew in abundance in the wild, and we knew the location of all the best blackberry patches. They usually came in season about early August. They were harvested and rendered into jelly, jam, and blackberry cobbler. Piping hot blackberry cobbler with a dollop or three of vanilla ice cream is one of God's special gifts to the human race. In addition to blackberries and elderberries they picked in the wild, my parents raised black raspberries. At one point, the raspberries were so prolific that they would sell them by the gallon. Besides homemade butter, black raspberry jam is probably the best friend a hot biscuit ever had.

We had a lot of variety in our diet. Sometimes we had soup beans, fried potatoes, and cornbread. Sometimes we had cornbread, fried potatoes, and soup beans. That's an exaggeration of course, but it is not an exaggeration to say that we ate a lot of soup beans, potatoes, and cornbread. Those were the workaday staples in our diet.

Sundays were different. After church we'd either go up to Grandma Hazel's or to our own house, and have a big, traditional Sunday dinner. Less often, we'd meet at Grandma Nell's, or maybe all three families would meet at our house. Dinner, by the way, is the meal that is eaten at noon. The evening meal is called supper. The four most exquisite words my large ears ever heard in those days were "Come on t' dinner!" especially when that dinner was on Sunday or a special occasion like Thanksgiving or Christmas.

Sunday dinner was pretty typical Southern fare, but extraordinarily good—fried chicken, biscuits, gravy, mashed potatoes, peas, and cake or pie or both for dessert. Sometimes we'd have oven-baked barbequed chicken, or maybe meatloaf, roast beef, or ham. Whatever it was that was served, it was delicious and plentiful.

Springtime afforded some special treats. Besides the approaching return of trout season in April, early to mid-March was ramp and branch lettuce season. A friend of mine from Minnesota said that when he moved South, he kept hearing about ramp festivals. Being from *the land of ten thousand lakes*, he eventually figured out that these festivities had nothing to do with boating. Bless hits heart!

For the uninitiated, a ramp, in the context of food, is a type of wild onion. Think of them as tiny green onions on steroids, with real bad attitudes. They are very pungent, like a combination of onions, garlic, and Lord knows what. When eaten raw, you don't want to be in close-quartered public places. I'm dead serious. Unless everyone eats them, and thus can't smell them on each other, they are very offensive.

When I was in elementary school, a brother and sister tandem, both of whom had been eating ramps, was sent home. Our little school was heated by steam. You can imagine the almost sickening odor of the ramps, conveyed by and mixed in with the steam. Always one to be frugal and creative, my very resourceful mother figured out that if you fry or boil ramps, or put them in soup, they weren't offensive at all.

Branch lettuce is a type of wild lettuce that matures about the same time as ramps. I don't know the official name for it. It has to be picked before it gets too big, or it's no good. It grows in rocky places in higher altitudes, near ice-cold spring water sources.

We knew where the favored places were for branch lettuce, some of which we called *lettuce rocks*. It's especially good as kilt lettuce. Kilt lettuce, whether branch lettuce or domestic leaf lettuce, is wilted via a combination of heated bacon or other grease, mixed with milk or buttermilk, and maybe some chopped ramps or green onions. That heated mixture is then poured over the lettuce. It's definitely *different,* but indescribably good.

A lot of poor unfortunate souls that I've met along my journey don't like soup beans. Honestly, in their defense, seeing the manner in which some people prepare them, I can understand a person's not liking them. Let's start with the bare basics. We'll call it *Soup Beans For People Who Don't Know Beans.*

First, the type of bean. The absolute best brown soup beans are Octobers, known also as cranberry beans. In my not-so-humble opinion, they're far better than pintos, of which I've eaten many. To me, comparing a pinto bean to a cranberry, would be like comparing a scooter to a Harley Davidson.

We occasionally had white beans too, usually navy beans, but Octobers were the chosen ones. Yellow eye beans were Grandpa Jack's favorites. We also ate shuck beans, referred to by some people as leather britches. They're dried-in-the-hull green beans that are strung up, and hung in a dry place. They turn tan (like leather), and are very brittle when they're dry, and are cooked hull and all, with a big chunk of fat back or streaked meat as seasoning.

Secondly, after soaking for several hours, then being rinsed, good soup beans have to be boiled very, *very* well. *Thoroughly.* Good soup beans—and I'm really passionate about this—*do not* rattle like marbles when they're spooned onto your plate or into your bowl. If they rattle, they're not done, and that's a big reason, I think, why so many detest them. Improperly cooked soup beans are hideous. You wouldn't eat rare or medium-rare chicken, would you? Unless you love salmonella-induced, projectile vomiting, my guess is no. Then who in God's wide world would like medium-rare soup beans? That's just not right! I'm crusading here for the dignity and glory of the humble brown bean.

You know that beans are cooked right when the water becomes a slightly thickened medium-brown. By definition, soup beans that are properly cooked don't display transparent liquid. If that were the case, they'd be called *broth beans* instead of by their proper name, *soup beans.*

Third, good beans have to be seasoned properly, and you have to add an adequate amount of salt. The seasoning of choice is either plain old fatback or streaked pork meat. A smoked ham bone is awfully good too, but those are few and far between, usually appearing only around holidays. In a pinch, bacon or bacon grease works just fine. I've even had them seasoned with creamy peanut butter. You don't taste the peanut butter.

And finally, really good soup beans require really good cornbread. And yes, I'm biased, but *really* good cornbread: (a) is not made from the contents of a packet or a box; (b) does not contain added sugar. It's one of life's mysteries to me why anyone would ruin cornmeal by adding sugar to it. If you're going to do that, then just serve your beans with a slab of pound cake and be done with it. Following in one of my uncle's footsteps, I do have to confess that I also like soup beans with a crumbled up cold biscuit, but at least it's not a sweet biscuit.

No one—not even my wife, my mother, or my paternal grandmother—could cook soup beans like my maternal grandmother, Grandma Hazel. No one in recorded history. Ever. She cooked the living daylights out of them. They were so rich and tasty. I always felt kind of sorry for my mother. Every time that she would cook a nice big pot of soup beans, she would ask me the same question: "Well, is them as good as Granny Hazel's?" It's not my fault that I was taught to tell the truth, and I would always answer my mother truthfully, usually with a simple, blunt "No." My mother was an incredible cook, and her soup beans were always First Runner Up, but as I said, no one on this or any other planet could fix them like Grandma Hazel. There was just something different about them, and I'm not entirely certain what it was.

It's 1967. I'm six years old, and in the first grade at Minneapolis Elementary School, seven miles from my home on Roaring Creek. It's dinner time, or lunch, as it was referred to at school. Soup beans and cornbread were served often in the school cafeteria at our little school of fewer than 200 students.

One particular day, early on in my first-grade year, soup beans were being served. I'll face God Almighty at the judgment, and I'm telling you the Gospel truth: when the good lunchroom lady spooned those beans into my melamine, blue-green, compartmented lunch plate, they rattled. I was mortified and traumatized. I was no chef, but I had enough experience with the fine art of beanology, and had eaten so many of Grandma Hazel's beans that, even at six, I knew soup beans weren't supposed to rattle when they hit your plate. Maybe readin', ritin', and 'rithmetic were not subjects that I had mastered at the time, but I did know beans. Panic and shock set in. I thought, "Dear God in heaven, what's the matter with them dadburned beans?!?"

I meant no disrespect to either of the lunchroom ladies, both wonderful people, but I decided to take it upon myself to pass along some valuable, albeit unsolicited advice, with the intention of being helpful. I said with utmost brassy conviction, "Youn's need fer my grandma to show youn's how to cook beans!" Yes, I really said that. Protocol be damned. It was dinner time, I was hungry, and they had spooned out into my plate what were supposed to be soup beans. One of the ladies, with a look of disbelief that a scrawny little Creeker had that level of audacity, said something to the effect that I was not being very nice or respectful, and maybe even ungrateful.

Maybe I should have dispensed my advice a bit differently, or maybe have said nothing at all. Yet, I maintained then, and even more so now, that good soup beans don't rattle when they hit your plate. I sincerely believed then and just as much now, that those ladies needed that kind of information. And while I'm finishing up on a roll here, you may as well know that their cornbread was dry and crumbly too. It's just not supposed to be that way.

Chapter 10: Gravy is My Favorite Beverage

After more than a half century of serious contemplation, I have decided that gravy is my favorite beverage. I used to maintain that there's no such thing as *bad* gravy, only *good* gravy and *better* gravy. Due to nearly six decades of experience, I've had to rethink and revise that conviction.

My family could make gravy out of practically anything except fried trout. Fish gravy just doesn't seem right even to mention in a sentence. Fish stew? Maybe, but not fish gravy. Almost anything else though, was fair game.

We made gravy out of the usual suspects: sausage gravy, bacon gravy, chicken gravy, roast beef gravy, etc. Then there were a few oddballs. Ever eat fried bologna gravy or hamburger gravy? How about chipped beef gravy? Some folks called chipped beef gravy by a different name, but this is a G-rated book. One company still markets dried beef in those little 4.5-ounce clear glass containers, which I think were the same size in the 60's and 70's. After emptying the contents, those ended up being drinking glasses, alongside my grandparents' snuff glasses. I still have some of them.

Out of the literally thousands of meals prepared by my mother, only a few stand out. That's sad to me, because as I've already indicated, she was an excellent cook. One of those standout meals was when a local hunter had given us a deer liver. For some reason, that liver had some attached pieces of lean muscle meat. Mommy trimmed off those pieces of lean venison, fried them (of course) and made gravy, biscuits, and the usual fixings.

I've learned that some things are so intensely personal, that people will come to blows if they feel like their sacred turf has been violated. I don't know if anyone ever got into a fight over gravy, but just like religion and politics, it is a very personal thing.

I do need to clarify a point or two at this juncture. *Real* gravy most definitely does not come out of a packet or a can. Some folks like brown gravy. I know I certainly do. Some folks like white gravy. I know I certainly do. There's milk gravy, water gravy (as in the kind made from cubed steak or roast beef drippings), and giblet gravy, which is essentially thickened turkey broth. I love 'em all. Most of 'em anyway.

There's also another gravy that I'm betting most of you have never heard of—chocolate gravy. Yes, that is a real thing. There were a few folks back home who made, and still make, a thin gravy out of cocoa powder, sugar, flour, and I'm not sure what else. You eat it over hot biscuits, like virtually any other kind of gravy, maybe even adding a dollop of butter. If there's anything that tastes better than that on a cold winter morning, then I'm not sure what it would be. It's tongue-beating-your-brains-out good!

About the only Southern Appalachian gravy that I can think of that I positively do not care for is red-eye gravy. I don't even consider it to be gravy. I think of it as *hillbilly au jus*. Red-eye gravy is a water-based, translucent, ultra-thin "gravy" (not really gravy), made from the drippings of country ham, with a little black coffee added for color. Red-eye gravy is like eating ham-colored water that is 67% sodium. It's so salty it makes anchovies taste bland by comparison. I don't like them either.

It'll probably cost me some Southern Appalachian credibility, but since I mentioned country ham, I don't really care for it. I know that'd be like someone from Louisiana saying that they don't like crawfish, but I'm just keeping it real here. I like everything about country ham except the way it tastes. It's just too briny for my delicate palate.

Texture is another thing that is very personal about gravy. The continuum runs from water-thin gravy (as I just discussed), to gravy thick enough to eat with a fork, and several viscosities in between. I'm definitely an in-between guy when it comes to gravy. Grandma Hazel made in-between white gravy. Grandma Nell made gravy the way Grandpa Rob liked it—the consistency of spackling paste. I can actually tolerate it that thick, but I prefer it in-between. I just like gravy… most of it.

One of the absolute best gravy bases comes from that old-timey, canned, ball sausage, sealed up in a pint jar. A single pint jar of that precious pig contains enough grease to keep a car lubricated for six months. And for the bravest of souls, besides the gravy, you eat the sausage balls. Afterwards, you find a comfortable spot and just sit really quiet and still for about an hour and let the grease settle.

Enough messing around. It's time to end the preliminaries and say what needs to be said. Among Creekers, and actually a lot of mountain folks elsewhere, the absolute gold standard when it comes to gravy is squirrel gravy. It is a little difficult to comprehend how an arboreal rodent can taste so good and, more importantly, make such divine gravy. Squirrel gravy is a white gravy, slightly on the thin side. Squirrel itself tastes a lot like (you know what I'm going to say) chicken. It honestly does. But the gravy has a distinct flavor that is very different from chicken gravy. About the only other competitor squirrel gravy has among us mountain folks is fresh, pork tenderloin gravy. But I don't think the bushy tails are in danger of being supplanted anytime soon.

I've strongly made the case already that my mother was a terrific country cook. However, she was mortal like the rest of us, and on extremely rare occasions, missed the boat. One day, my wife, daughter, sister Donna, and I were breaking bread at my mother's table. As I recall, this was not too terribly long before she passed in 2012. She served meatloaf that day. I adore meatloaf. My favorite thing about meatloaf is the days after it's initially served, eating cold meatloaf sandwiches on white bread with a lot of mayonnaise.

Along with that meatloaf, my mother did something that is beyond my powers of explanation. She decided to serve gravy, which I'd normally say is a splendid decision, but she made it from the drippings of that meatloaf. Picture the University of Texas burnt orange-colored gravy. Not white gravy. Not brown gravy. Not in-between tan gravy, but burnt orange gravy. It was orange from the tomato sauce and ketchup in the meatloaf, with a hint of onion, garlic, and enough salt for a livestock lick.

On that infamous, burnt-orange gravy day, I did taste the gravy so as not to offend my mother. However, from that day forward until the present, I no longer boldly assert that there's no such thing as bad gravy. Bad gravy *does indeed* exist, but given the great, the good, the bad, and the downright bizarre, it's still my favorite beverage.

Chapter 11: Meat Don't Come from A Store

Warning: if you are one of those people who likes to pretend that meat comes from a magical cooler in retail stores, or if you have a squeamish constitution, you might want to skip this chapter. Despite some of my foolishness and hyperbole, I am being completely serious. Proceed at your own risk. You have been warned. If, on the other hand, you appreciate realism and utter transparency, you'll appreciate this chapter.

Growing up on a small farm, I learned from a very young age that you don't name your animals that you intend to use as food sources. Something with a name ceases to be livestock, and has transitioned over into pet status. Horses, mules, and of course, dogs and cats had names, but they weren't table fare.

Speaking of names, most of our dogs were named Spot. We even had a longhaired cat named Spot. That cat was solid white, and was sometimes called Fluffy, probably because it was so circumferentially challenged, or maybe because it looked like a fluffy cloud. The more I thought about it, the more sense it made that its other name was Spot. The physical sum total of that solid white cat in question, actually made a big white spot. Rhyme and reason were thus in play.

When I was a wee lad up to about, I think nine or ten, we, like a lot of mountain families, kept a milk cow. Sometimes I'd go up in the pasture and drive her down to the house so that my mother could milk her. Our milk cows were usually Jerseys or Guernseys, and tended to be kind and gentle souls. They were a vital mainstay in the food supply chain. No wonder the Hindus revere cattle.

Besides the drinking milk the cows supplied, there was the buttermilk, and that incredibly rich, home-churned butter. My mother had one of those wooden butter molds with a clover leaf design that made an impression in the cake of butter.

Whatever milk that might have gotten left over from the daily milking, that didn't end up as drinking milk, buttermilk, or butter, would go to the hogs in the form of, well, *slop*. Slop is an unflattering, nasty-sounding term that is used to describe a concoction of milk, bread, leftover vegetables, leftover table scraps, with maybe some livestock chop added. Trust me, hogs love slop, and do they ever grow fast on it. I've never met a hog with a picky appetite.

Another fact I learned very early was where meat came from. Decidedly, it did not come from a store. For many families on the Creek, like mine, besides the vegetables and fruits that we either ate fresh, canned, dried, or frozen, home grown chickens, home grown eggs, and home-grown pork were staples. For most families, pork was the preferred protein. I myself preferred beef, and still do, but pork was the winter mainstay.

In my formative years, I don't ever remember my family not raising at least one hog per year. On occasion, we raised two. We didn't name them Arnold, Babe, or Porky. We didn't name them anything. We treated them humanely, and they had a very nice, large lot in which to roam freely, and a pen to shelter them from the elements. But they were in our care for a specific reason, and their days were numbered. They were *not* to be named.

Usually in the Spring, daddy would buy a young pig from one of our local men like cousin Clayton Hughes or Herman Buchanan, the latter of which lived in the Minneapolis area. If it happened to be a boar, it had to be "changed" (that's what they called it) or neutered. It wasn't done by a vet. While the young male pig was being held, screaming an ear-splitting high G, one of the experienced men would simply use his very sharp pocket knife, remove the testicles, then smear some sort of blue disinfectant on the incision. I don't ever remember a boar pig or bull calf getting an infection from what probably sounds like a very crude, harsh procedure. Folks did what they knew to do, what they had to do, and made do with what they had.

Typically, late November to early December was hog-killing time. From early Spring to that timeframe, what started out as a 50 to 60-pound pig was now in the vicinity of 350 to 400 pounds. We wanted them just big enough, but not massive, as in the 700-800-pound range. We raised several different breeds of hogs over the years, including Yorkshires (plain white), Hampshires (black with a white band around the shoulders and front legs), and Tamworths (red). The white ones were probably the easiest to scrape clean during processing time, but we would buy and raise whatever happened to be available from the peddlers.

A cold, dry, crisp Saturday was the chosen day for hog-killing. Daddy was off work, and several other men would come and help, usually relatives. I can still smell the scent of kerosene-doused kindling wood, as a fire was lit beneath the 50-gallon barrel of water. The water had to be heated to scalding—not boiling—temperature.

A special assortment of tools would be gathered—long, stiff-bladed knives, the style of which was somewhere between machetes and large butcher knives (used for scraping); burlap sacks (for the scalding process); a razor-sharp axe or hatchet or both (for cutting through bone); block and tackle (for hoisting the carcass).

Once the water in the 50-gallon drum reached its proper temperature, there was one more piece of equipment that had to brought to the big curly maple tree, down in the hog lot, behind the hog pen, beside the creek—a .22 rifle capable of firing a .22 short cartridge. A .22 short is among, if not, the least powerful of all cartridges, but highly effective for the task ahead. It was time.

In the sharp early morning November or December air, with frost or snow crunching beneath out work boots, a small door to the hog pen would be opened. The hog might be coaxed out of its pen with some sort of food. Once the hog became sufficiently interested in what was before it, its head pointed slightly downward, with the rifle barrel nearly touching the forehead, a dull SPAT, no louder than a quick handclap, shattered the morning silence. Ideally, there would be only one well-placed, point-blank shot that would penetrate the hog's skull between the eyes, enter the brain, and painlessly render the animal lifeless in a matter of seconds.

The rifle shot was the most intense, solemn moment of the day. It needed to be done humanely, correctly, and as quickly as possible. As soon as the hog was deemed legitimately dead, a sharp knife would find the jugular vein for the messy but very necessary bleeding out.

Grandma Nell told me that some of her relatives used to catch the gushing hog blood in a pan when the jugular was severed, to make blood pudding. I have never even seen blood pudding, much less tried it. Several years ago, one of my students in the community college where I teach said it was pretty good. Can you guess where she was from? The British Isles. Yet another fleeting glimpse into the traditions of my ancestors.

It was now time for the grueling, day's-long work to begin. The hog would be dragged from its pen to beneath the hard maple tree, later to be used for hoisting. It was then turned onto one side. Burlap sacks would be placed on the carcass, which would serve to soak up the scalding water, which was slowly and methodically poured over the sacks. The combination of wet burlap, and scalded hog bristles is not a scent I'll ever forget. After a few minutes, the sacks were removed, and the scraping to remove the bristles would begin. The men were expert at this, as they had done it scores of times. As a boy, I watched, learned, and jumped right in like an old hand, avoiding the harder areas, leaving them for the more experienced hands. We scraped every part—sides, belly, back, legs, shoulders, hams, feet, and even the ears, tail, and head.

After what seemed like a long and tedious process, it was time to hoist the hog. The hooks of the gambrel were placed in a slit that had been cut between the Achille's tendons and ankle bones of the rear feet. Those tendons are incredibly strong. "Pull! Heave! Pull! Heave! Make sure the upper pulley block is locked! Now tie off that rope around the big maple tree!" The hog's nose would clear the ground by only a few inches, but that was plenty. The carcass would then be thoroughly cleansed by buckets of cold water from the creek right beside us. Any visible dirt, debris, or stray bristles would be removed. The actual butchering was ready to begin.

Starting at the underside nearest the tail, a sharp knife would make an incision down the length of the hog's body. There was a lot of fat to get through, but the abdominal wall had to be cut, being ever so careful not to nick an intestine. The intestines and the rest of the entrails were removed and kept separate. There was more to be done with the intestines later. The only internal part we ate was the liver. If you've never had fresh, homemade livermush, you have missed a delicacy. If, however, you don't like liver, then that's a moot point. I'm a little surprised that we didn't eat the heart, but we didn't. I don't think we used it for anything, unless it became part of the sausage.

Like his father, Grandpa 'Field would eat anything. He would even eat the lights, i.e., the lungs. I tried a single bite of lung one time, and…it took my breath away (bad pun intended). It was like eating a rubbery cleaning sponge, soaked in grease.

Maybe it would be more accurate to say that I ate lung meat twice in one meal: my first time and my last time! Other than chicken gizzards, and clams, I don't like anything that bites back when you try to eat it.

After all the entrails were removed, the head was carefully removed and safely hung on a nail on one of the nearby trees. The front feet, the shoulders, the loins, the belly fat, and finally the hams, the rear feet, and the backbone and ribs were separated out. Some parts, like the shoulders for example, would be ground into sausage. The backbone and the ribs would be portioned out. As a meal, they would be parboiled together with Irish potatoes, in a dish we simply referred to as *backbones and ribs*. The hams would be either sugar cured or salt cured, and the fatback and streaked meat would be salt cured. All were placed in a safe, clean, rat-free place in the coolness of the barn loft. The feet, the tail, and even the ears would be well-cleaned, and used as part of our meals.

As is usually the case, the women had one of the hardest jobs of the day. They painstakingly cut off every bit of the delicate, white, visceral fat attached to the intestines. It has a different look and texture from other fat. It would then be rendered into pure, white lard to be used for shortening, and placed in metal coffee cans with lids, both of which had been saved up throughout the year. Any little piece of lean meat that didn't cook down into lard would be canned separately. Those pieces were called cracklings. Added to cornbread mixture, cracklings are one of cornbread's best friends. I'm a little surprised that we didn't eat chitterlings/chit'lins but we didn't. Those are the small intestines themselves. I've tried them, and liked them.

The head was a special delicacy for a future get-together. It would be boiled whole in a large pot, minus the eyes, the nostrils, and ears, and was a multi-family affair. My wife had never seen hog's head served as the main entrée, before she married me. One day, we went up to my folks for supper, and a great big pot was simmering on the stove. She lifted the lid, and was taken aback to see a huge head with empty eye sockets staring back at her! Nothing says "Welcome to Roaring Creek" like a simmering hog's head. She did well for a pretty, delicate, uninitiated gal, but neither that day up until the present has she ever tried hog's head.

The head is mostly fat, but there are a few lean morsels, and the best part is the brain. After all the edible portions were cleaned off, we'd take a large stiff knife and pop open the well-cooked skull. Some people like brains and scrambled eggs.

The remaining portions from the head, whether fat or lean, would be turned into what we called *souse meat*. Some folks call the same dish *head cheese*. Souse is a gelatinous, pickled dish that is served as a side dish or snack. I liked it fairly well. It tasted kind of like pickled pig's feet, except it was pickled pig's head, or something like that.

My mother loved the obscure parts—the feet, the ears, and the tail. I can honestly say that I've never tried the latter two, but I loved parboiled pig's feet. I had no idea that ligaments tasted so good, and that's mostly what they are. Pig's "feet" is really something of a misnomer, because it's mostly pig's ankles, but nobody calls them that. It's like eating a rich, savory, greasy combination of rubber bands, gristle, and white glue.

In my estimation, the crème de la crème in the tasty world of hogdom is the tenderloin. Sometimes, either the same evening on which we butchered the hog, or maybe the next morning, we'd have fresh, fried tenderloin with biscuits, gravy, eggs, grits, hashbrowns, jelly, and jam. Tenderloin gravy is right up there near or at the very top of the gravyometer.

We worked hard, not just on hog-killing day, but there was a satisfaction in what we did. It wasn't the kind of mind-numbing, monotonous cubicle work that makes you wonder if it really means anything. We touched, saw, and tasted our work. It had purpose, rhyme, reason. If some of our practices seemed crude or harsh, and even if our fare may have seemed shocking or repulsive to some, we knew where our food came from, and how it came to be in the first place. Simply put, that worked for us.

When mommy would send me to the cellar to fetch a pint jar of sausage, or a quart jar of sauerkraut, or a bowl of potatoes out of the potato bin; or when daddy would slice some of the cured ham stored in the barn and bring it into the kitchen, we never had to wonder how long it'd been on a store shelf, or how it was processed, or if was safe. We enjoyed and survived on the fruit of our labor. I'm profoundly thankful that I never for a moment thought that meat and vegetables just magically appeared in the coolers and on the shelves of our local grocers. Knowing, I can never unknow. I'm glad I know.

Chapter 12: Beyond the Frown

It would be ludicrous to presume to pen a memoir without breaching the all-important, ever-controversial topic of religion. Everyone—from hard-left atheist to hellfire-right fundamentalist—has strong opinions about religion. It's only partially facetious for me to say that if you were to put five very devoutly religious people in the same room, you'd have at least seven different opinions.

Both by practice and by professional training, my entire life has been lived in and around matters religious. That being the case, I knew that I would either have to include more than one chapter on religion, or vigorously apply the brakes and not attempt to cover a 42-acre field of history, theology, ethics, and personal experience. After all, I do want you to finish this book!

I think it would be safe and reasonable to say that everyone on Roaring Creek had and still has a religious consciousness. I don't mean to suggest that all are religious practitioners per sé, but there is a strong religious/spiritual awareness.

A few years ago, I had a rental guest staying at my Roaring Creek home place. We happened to be talking on the phone one day when he said, "There must not be any sin in this community!" I, of course, asked why he would say that. He said, as many have noted, that there are three churches in the community, all in close proximity to each other. Thus, the no-sin deduction. There are indeed three churches, serving a community of approximately 300, but I'm pretty sure that there's sin aplenty.

It is only logical that I can't talk about religion without at least touching on the subjects of morals and ethics. Among many, there's a hierarchy in morality. It goes something like: "I may have done X, but at *least* I've never done Y!" I am told, and hope never to find out personally, that this hierarchy is quite evident among those incarcerated in prison. Certain crimes are deemed more heinous than others, and those who have allegedly committed such crimes are treated more severely by the prison population.

Roaring Creek was and is no Puritanical community. There was a great deal that went on, generally spoken of in very hushed tones, if mentioned at all. For example, there were numerous moonshiners, closet alcoholics, and participants in blood sports. No one seemed alarmed—live and let live.

Back to the hierarchy of morality, it's really interesting that perhaps the majority of the community, including me in my early years, used tobacco in some form or another—cigarettes, snuff, or chewing tobacco—and no one dreamed of associating it with any moral breach whatsoever. After all, it was North Carolina, and tobacco was considered to be one of the basic food groups. Alcohol, however, was certain to damn your soul, according to conventional wisdom and dogma. And it was perfectly acceptable to use four-letter words, so long as God's name wasn't used.

As I got older, I realized that some children didn't look like their parents. Deciphering some of the hushed tones, I learned that some folks' parents really *weren't* their biological parents. The biggest difference in terms of questionable morality between then and now is that then, it was either covered up or not discussed, now we go on national television and tell everyone. Oh well, they may have done X, but *at least* they didn't do Y. The hierarchy of morals was thus displayed in all its glory.

In the interest of necessary context, I simply must ask for your patience for a short history lesson. As noted elsewhere in the book, Roaring Creek Missionary Baptist Church, the very first church in the community, was founded in 1871. It was founded by our first white settler, Jeremiah Hughes, and a preacher Cook from over in Cane Creek in Mitchell County. Because Great Grandfather, Rev. Garfield Hughes, was such a fixture in the community, and preached and pastored for about fifty-something years, both at Roaring Creek and elsewhere, some have mistakenly thought that he was the church's first pastor. 1871 was eleven years before Grandpa 'Field was even born. Great Grandpa 'Field's Uncle Sanders Hughes, son of Jeremiah, was the first pastor of Roaring Creek Missionary Baptist Church.

For what it's worth, there are literally scores, some say hundreds, of different types of Baptists. Throughout much of the South, there are probably more Baptists than there are people. Some Missionary Baptist churches became part of the Southern Baptist Convention (est. 1845), the largest Baptist body in the world, and also the largest Protestant denomination. Roaring Creek was thus affiliated until the early 1970's, before becoming independent of any larger Baptist denominational body.

Here's where things get interesting, or maybe even confusing, but the adjective *Missionary,* attached to Baptist, further identifies which type of Baptist group we're talking about. Missionary Baptists, being differentiated from Primitive or Hardshell Baptists, distinguish themselves with an emphasis on human will and personal response to the gospel, and the need to support missionaries among various unreached people groups. I could say much more along these lines but it would create a detour, and perhaps a convoluted one at that. I'll resist the lecture-mode urge.

Sometime in the 1930's, a split occurred in Roaring Creek Missionary Baptist Church. A group led by preachers of Freewill Baptist persuasion, who place even more emphasis on human will than the Missionary Baptists, broke away and founded their own congregation about a quarter of a mile down the road. There's not 14¢ worth of difference between the two. The major differences pertain to the "once-saved-always-saved" belief, held by Missionary Baptists, and the number of prescribed church ordinances. Unlike the Missionary Baptists, the Freewill Baptists hold that a person can forfeit his/her salvation. And Missionary Baptists practice only two church ordinances: believers' baptism by full immersion, and the Lord's Supper or Holy Communion. In addition to those two ordinances, Freewill Baptists add a third, foot-washing. Other than maybe some stylistic differences, those are the major ones.

In 1962, a Pentecostal Holiness church, The People's Church, was formed, and it was about a quarter of a mile up the road from the Missionary Baptist Church. Their worship was lively, loud, and jubilant. How dare they have fun in church! Besides a piano and organ, they incorporated both electric and acoustic stringed instruments, along with drums and tambourines. One fellow said after he attended a worship service there, "…that was the purttiest rock 'n roll music you ever hyerd!"

Among the three churches, we practiced mutual respect and co-existence long before it was cool and politically correct, and mostly avoided any holy wars of words or otherwise. I'm happy to report that as of this writing, there's probably more of a mutual spirit of love and cooperation among the three than there ever has been. At least now you know why Roaring Creek community has three churches. Thank you for your patience, let's move on now.

My parents and I attended the Missionary Baptist Church. My brother and sisters had attended most of the time until they moved away. Eventually, mommy, daddy, and I became at-church-every-time-the-door-is-open kind of people. I don't remember our being there for three services a week in my single-digit years, but along the way that changed some time or another. My parents, especially my mother, were very duty-driven people. We didn't necessarily feel that we had to like it or feel that it was always of great spiritual benefit, we just did it. It was expected, and it was our duty.

The tiny Missionary Baptist Church was a congregation of about sixty. It wasn't an atypical Missionary Baptist Church at all. Like many of the Baptist churches in the area, we sang from *Church Hymnal,* aka the *Red Hymnal.*

In my home church, as in many of that day in our area, and even in the present day, the King James Version of the Bible was regarded as the *only* legitimate version of the Bible. Any other version was dubbed unfit for human consumption, and warranted divine disapproval. No one bothered to explain why there were scores of English translations *before* the initial version of the KJV in 1611, or that the KJV 1611 underwent several revisions *after* 1611. "King James-onlyism" is something of a fundamentalist sub-culture within fundamentalism. By no means are all Christian fundamentalists King James-only. Roaring Creek Missionary Baptist, however, was and still is King James-only.

Seeing that I wasn't even in my double-digits in terms of age, I have only vague memories of Grandpa 'Field as pastor of the Missionary Baptist Church. I do have a pretty good recollection of those pastors who followed him though.

From what I remember, and have heard, Grandpa 'Field wasn't a preacher given to scare tactics. In the mountain culture, Roaring Creek certainly being no exception, fear and shame were frequently utilized as key motivators of what was considered to be accepted belief and behavior. This was true not only in the church setting, but also in many homes. It seemed to be the goal of many of the preachers in my childhood and adolescence to get you to heaven by scaring the hell out of you!

Not very far into my adolescence, in the mid-1970's, "gospel films" became very popular. They were shown in local churches, usually Baptist. I remember a certain warm summer day, going to Bob Burleson's store. As I started to walk in, a colorful poster taped to the plate glass window, to the left of the door, caught my eye. It depicted some poor tortured soul roasting in flames, obviously not being consumed. I don't remember everything on the poster, but one of the captions mesmerized me. It read "20,000 degrees Fahrenheit and not a drop of water!" It was advertising a showing of *The Burning Hell* at one of the churches in the area. I had barely enough critical capacity to do so, but I did wonder exactly how anyone knew the temperature of hell.

Eventually, *The Burning Hell* was shown at my home church. To a fourteen-year-old who had been largely insulated from the harsh realities of the world, it was a pretty dadgum scary film. At the end, of course, an "altar call" or "invitation" was given for any who felt the need to respond. My good buddy, Leo Hicks, nudged me in the ribs and said, "Come on! Let's go up!" I honestly didn't feel the need to "go up," but I went up with Leo just in case. I guess I figured it wouldn't hurt for one to review his or her fire insurance policy.

The ultimate goal of revivalist preachers in my boyhood years was to get people to respond to what they deemed as that all-important altar call or invitation. If, at the conclusion of the sermon, folks weren't responding to the altar call like the preachers felt that they should, there were three very effective stock in trade tools they used to shake people to their core.

First, it was common among those aforementioned preachers to resort to terrifying deathbed stories of people who purportedly died and went to hell. At least that's where they went according to those types of preachers. Some of those hellfire and brimstone preachers spoke of hell as if they had personally conducted tours of it.

To make matters really terrifying, in many of those stories, the dying person was a faithful church member, who only *thought* that he/she was saved. While on their deathbed, as their life ebbed away, they realized, albeit too late, that they really weren't saved after all. Even though, according to the tellers of some of these stories, the poor miserable, terrified souls begged God for saving mercy, it was too late for saving grace. God had abandoned them, and they slipped away into a pitch-dark, sulfurous, burning hell, where they would remain forever and ever with no possibility of parole.

A second tool in the revivalist preachers' repertoire utilized another very troubling theme to which they referred as *sinning away your day of grace*. That's revivalist "preacher talk" for a common belief in certain circles that holds that every person has only a set number of times in which God will deal with them in order to persuade them to be saved. For some, it might be two dozen or two hundred times, and for others it might be only a time or two. No one knows. If a person is unfortunate enough to cross that invisible deadline, or "sin away their day of grace," at that point, there is absolutely no possibility that such a one can ever be saved. They had reached their expiration date. No more opportunities. Eternally doomed.

If that weren't scary enough, sometimes the preachers would stop and point either to their left or right and say something like "God has impressed it upon my heart that there's someone on my right (or left), and this is the last time that God will ever deal with you to be saved! If you leave this building tonight, you'll never be saved!" I'm positive that that one got me up out of my pew and down to the front many times.

One more tool of terror that was devastatingly effective was the subject of *the rapture of the church.* A common belief in my formative spiritual sphere was that of the rapture. The rapture teaching was understood as a sudden, surprise event in which all living Christians would be caught up or "raptured" before the dreadful seven-year Great Tribulation. Along with the living Christians, deceased Christians would be raised from the dead, and the living and the resurrected would have a blessed meeting in the air. If you were one of the ones left behind, God have mercy on you. It was generally assumed that if anyone previously had an opportunity to be saved, and didn't take advantage of it, they were not only doomed to suffer the seven-year period of global tribulation, but also would be cast into the lake of fire and brimstone at the end of time. It was *lose, lose* either way. For clarity's sake, I myself do not hold to this doctrine as I was first taught.

Let me share a combination that will yield years or even decades of psychological trauma, depression, and anxiety: take one hormonal, adolescent boy; give him a high level of thoughtfulness and conscientiousness; do everything you can in a religious context to create fear, guilt, shame, doubt, and anxiety; and then teach him that the Bible means exactly what it says, and says exactly what it means, in the most absolute sense, and that if he ever questions one word therein that he's ever been taught, then it just proves he was never really a true Christian to begin with. That is a reliable combination that will wreak havoc without fail. Many nights I would awake with cold sweat on my brow, deeply distressed, despite everything in my faith and experience, that maybe I really wasn't saved, maybe I've crossed that invisible deadline, maybe the rapture has occurred tonight and I've been left behind.

I feel incredibly blessed that I was not/am not as many who have suffered complete mental breakdowns over these matters. A good Christian psychologist friend of mine told me of a lady who suffered a complete mental breakdown after having experienced some of the same things that I described. Her breaking point was one of those "gospel films." She is but one of many who suffered such a breakdown. Surely, if anything breaks the heart of the merciful Father, that would be it.

Let me assure you of something in no uncertain terms, despite some of my foolishness and tongue-in-cheek humor. After more than six decades of up-close and personal religious experience, there's not an iota of humor in the matters I have just breached. It never has been, and never will be the least bit funny to me. The redeeming virtue in all of this, however, has been my being able to help others still trapped in this vicious cycle of religious and emotional trauma, and who have had little to no exposure to solid Biblical teaching.

In those formative, impressionable years, I often heard preachers reference the love of God, the substitutionary death of Jesus for non-Christians, and the grace of God. And I listened. I didn't merely occupy a pew for an hour or so, then simply check it off as just another Sunday morning, another Sunday evening, another Wednesday prayer meeting, or any other church gathering. I listened. I absorbed it. I studied and memorized the "proof-texts." I knew the correct definitions.

In that spiritual environment, unless I had been some sort of child prodigy, which I was not, there was little to no likelihood in those tender years that I would have had the critical faculties to evaluate the things I heard, experienced, and witnessed. In retrospect, I now realize that there were a bunch of dots that simply didn't connect for me. That is a realization to which I would have never admitted back in the day.

It is well-nigh impossible, to my mind anyway, to comprehend that God is presumably a God of love, when the person conveying that message is yelling at you in deafening decibels, is drenched in sweat, has a flushed face, and seems to be very angry. That was a total disconnect, but I knew not to question it. I assumed that the problem must have been with me.

"Touch not the LORD's anointed, and do my prophets no harm..." was an oft-repeated, ingrained dictum, invisibly chiseled in granite. What the preacher said was surely infallible, and you best not question it, unless you want God to strike you dead. To hear on one hand that God is gracious and merciful, and yet be constantly bombarded with the unspoken message that God is extremely angry, and not to be provoked by even the slightest misstep, and will indeed roast the majority of the human race in a literal burning furnace of fire, led only to more disconnect.

One of the most heart-rending memories I have, religious or otherwise, was born out of a mid-morning conversation I had with my mother. It was some time in 1989, shortly after the tragic passing of my sister, Pam. At the homeplace, my mother and I were sitting on the back deck that overlooks the creek. It was a beautiful summer morning. Despite our faithfulness to the church, my parents and I had very few conversations that directly breached the topic of religion and matters of faith. It was one of several *unspokens* within my family.

I decided to go for broke and ask my mother—the very woman who bore me, the one who taught me more than anyone—a deep, philosophical/theological question. Knowing that Pam was the third-deceased of six children, I decided that my mother would surely have some very substantial, deep concepts of God, and would undoubtedly possess a treasure trove of godly wisdom. So, I asked, "What is your concept of God?" Bracing myself for her answer, I was honestly expecting thunder and lightning. Her reply was, "I'm afraid of God."

To understate it severely, I was disappointed in my mother's answer. More than merely disappointed, I was heartbroken. My precious mother—well into her sixties by that time, faithful, godly churchwoman her entire life, as morally upright as a person could be, supporter of the church and her pastor, both in presence and pocketbook, avid reader, great mind—afraid of God. Not merely in *awe of* God, or having a deep, reverential trust, but afraid. Not merely disappointed in the actions of God, not daring even for a second to raise the "why" question toward God, not merely uncomfortable or hurt at God, but *afraid* of God. I honestly believe that Father God wept at that moment.

My mother was a product of her religious environment. But that moment was a crystal-clear window into a religious interpretation, both of Scripture and life, that I now believe to be weighed in the balances and found wanting in terms of grace, mercy, love, compassion, and wholesome teaching. I hope she heard what Donna and I said to her as she lay dying. Minutes before she passed, we were holding her hand, and we told her not to be afraid, that God is merciful and gracious, and loves her so very much.

How well I remember an incident when I was in the eighth grade. It is one that paints an unmistakable portrait of where I once was, and where I would remain, to varying degrees, for close to another decade afterwards. I was fourteen at the time. It was lunch time at Minneapolis Elementary. I could take you within three inches of the exact spot where it happened. One of the pretty girls in my class was walking past me there in the lunchroom. Sounding half angry and half concerned she said, "Chris, what's *wrong* with you? You seem so depressed!" I brushed it off saying something like "Nothing! I'm fine!" I wasn't fine. I honestly thought that. Truth be told, I was far from fine. It was my "normal," simply the way I had begun to function and feel, a couple of years before that day.

I should have been thinking about gorgeous girls in my same grade (like the one who asked me that question), going fishing after school, working on improving my jump shot, where I wanted to go camping on Friday night, or a dozen other things. Nope. Not me. I really was deeply depressed and highly concerned that maybe I really wasn't a Christian at all. She nailed me with her pointed question.

At the time of course, I didn't know that's what depression was, how it made you feel, or even how it made you look to an observant classmate. "It," i.e., low-grade depression, became my *normal* for years to come. Mental health specialists used to refer to that type of depression as dysthymia, now it's usually just called low-grade depression. The person afflicted with it is functional, generally appears to be OK, but nevertheless is depressed.

Lest there be any misconceptions, I want it clearly understood, that the spiritual and emotional trauma of those uneasy years was not directly and intentionally inflicted on me by my parents. Sadly, some who were/are in that boat cannot say the same. My parents were actually pretty moderate folks in demeanor, dogma, and praxis. I relinquish them of any accusation or association with regard to my own history. Their spiritual assumptions were not of their own making. They did what they knew to do under the circumstances with which they were conversant. My own experiences and internal wiring were separate from theirs, and truthfully, from that of most others. Most people in my religious environment did not have the same reaction as I. There's no finger-pointing here, just personal transparency.

I'm not about to end a chapter on religion on a sour note. Despite some negative aspects, and serious ones at that, there were also some very positive ones. Every aspect of life is a mixture of negative and positive—family, work, play, and yes, spirituality. Why should I or anyone else idealize religion as something completely positive? The negative is as necessary as the positive. All sunshine makes deserts.

Believing in giving honor to those to whom honor is due, I must pay tribute to two individuals whose spiritual influence on my life looms largely. In my early to late teens, there were two different pastors of my home church, both of whom left indelible impressions on my life in very different ways. Not only were the impressions different, but the men themselves were, in most ways, polar opposites. They were both "old school" preachers, but they expressed their "schooling" differently.

The first was Rev. Park Whitson. I'll start by delineating what Park was *not*. He wasn't a great preacher. He was not a riveting, insightful teacher. He had no formal divinity training. He wasn't young and energetic, didn't have a great sense of humor, or a dynamic personality. He didn't live in the community, a fact not uncommon for rural pastors of small churches in those days, and somewhat for these days as well.

Notwithstanding the negatives, there were several indisputable positives for Pastor Whitson. He was utterly sincere, genuinely caring, devout, morally upright, and dead serious about the faith. Those qualities matter. They matter a lot. Those facts were not lost on me.

I've absolutely no doubt that were he still living, Pastor Whitson and I would differ on a wide range of faith issues, and perhaps other issues as well. That *doesn't* matter. Differences aside, the shadow he cast over me was long, and he became a major influence.

The second pastor was Rev. Dana Williams. In 1976, I had just turned sixteen when Pastor Williams became our pastor, he being only twenty-two. My home church was his first pastorate. Originally hailing from West Virginia, and later Cleveland, Ohio, he adjusted remarkably well to an infinitely slower pace of life to which he had grown accustomed in Cleveland, and to our very different dialect, and our 'quare' mountain ways.

Pastor Williams was a dynamic preacher, a persuasive teacher, and the first pastor we ever had with some formal theological training. He was energetic, funny, and had a winning personality. Living right beside the church in our newly acquired parsonage, he was the first pastor with whom I became close friends. He was actually my pastor twice: once at Roaring Creek, and once at another church in the area.

On the rare occasions that we see each other now, Pastor Williams won't let me forget something. With just a tad of mild resentment, he reminds me of how his wife, Esther, would always make sure that I got the biggest steak whenever I'd eat with them, which was actually pretty often. I can't help it that steering a young man into the ministry can be a pretty costly and sacrificial investment.

The most significant impact that Pastor Williams made on my life was through my friendship with him, his wife, and his four then-young children. That friendship played an enormous role in helping me overcome some of my fears, misconceptions, and uneasiness in regard to the Christian faith.

Again, divergent paths and points of view do not matter at this particular intersection. The power of positive influence can and should supersede mostly peripheral differences among individuals.

Fundamentalist Christianity contributed to my academic interests. I have no doubt that some of you read that sentence twice—*fundamentalist* and *academic* used in the same sentence? Yes. Here's why. Fundamentalism insists on a very wooden, literal, black and white approach to matters spiritual, moral, and ethical. Overly literal and rigid sometimes— absolutely—but it helped me to take spiritual matters more seriously than I might have otherwise. I neither regret nor resent that. I've learned that nothing in our life experiences is wasted, and to use the lessons, techniques, and tools at my disposal.

Some of the most rigid fundamentalists I've ever known, in a manner of speaking, are atheists, agnostics, and Christian liberals. Such sometimes cloak their fundamentalism in intellectual garb, but it's still fundamentalism. Just because I no longer identify as a fundamentalist Christian does not mean that I see no redeeming virtue in it, or that I view it as a one-dimensional entity.

My faith community grounded me not only in ecclesiastical and spiritual matters, but also provided me with a social matrix as well. The bond was strong, tight, authentic. We all need a tribe. In my formative years, the church was my most significant tribe, because it incorporated what for me are three of my top values: faith, family, belonging.

The church gave me a moral compass. I had to develop most of my critical (critical in this context refers to skillful discernment and close scrutiny) and analytical faculties on my own, but that's just part of what growing up is all about. At least I had some sort of moral/spiritual infrastructure from which to proceed.

I sometimes illustrate religious or other experience with eating a big, juicy slice of watermelon. I personally spit out the seeds and eat the rest. There are "seeds" in anything. I eventually figured out that it is perfectly acceptable to step back and critique one's upbringing, beliefs, and experience, and then make the necessary adjustments.

As a sort of passing-the-torch-moment, I suppose I need to mention my own call to the ministry. Over the years, people have asked me "How did you know that you were called to preach?" Well, it was like this. One Monday morning, after a particularly good day at church the day before, I woke up craving fried chicken, and didn't want to go to work. I've actually said this to some people, but it was a little more substantial than that. OK, a *lot more* substantial.

117

The short version of "how did I know?" is that it was virtually a default awareness. I began teaching adult and youth Sunday School when I was about twelve. That's *much* too young, and I am aware of that, but mountain churches are different in a number of ways. For me, "the call" wasn't a cataclysmic moment like the conversion of Saul of Tarsus, or Martin Luther's life-altering thunderstorm, but a gradual impression and a growing sense of finding my niche.

In my home church, not a single soul registered any sort of surprise or excitement when I made my call public. I was licensed and ordained to the ministry at age twenty. Again, way too young, but I can't un-ring that bell.

I did understand clearly, a few years after my ordination, as a much-too-young pastor, that there were very legitimate reasons why Jewish rabbis did not begin their public ministry until they were at least thirty years of age. Even Jesus didn't go public with His ministry until He was thirty. We live, and hopefully, we learn.

In March 1979, I stood beside my Great Grandfather, Rev. Garfield Hughes, as he lay on his death bed, in his own home. He was 97 at the time of his death, and was as lucid and sharp as ever up until the very final days of his being bed-bound for only two weeks. He told me something that I appreciate much more now than then, as an 18-year-old. He told me that he had prayed for years for someone in the Hughes generation to be raised up by God to take his place. He said that for a long time he thought it was his grandson, my Uncle Curt. He then said that he now believed instead that that someone was me.

That moment was like an old Bible patriarch who, just prior to his departure, pronounced a blessing on his sons. It was a far more significant and special moment than I realized at the time. I would never presume, however, that I could ever "take his place."

William Cowper (1731-1800) was a true, dark blue melancholic. He suffered from severe clinical depression and doubt. Not in the least surprisingly, I am irresistibly drawn to him and his ilk. At one time, he was institutionalized for insanity. In 1773, the same year as one of several of his suicide attempts, Cowper penned a poem entitled *Light Shining Out of Darkness*. This poem became the basis for the famous hymn and common expression, *God Moves in a Mysterious Way*. One of the stanzas in the poem/song says:

Judge not the Lord by feeble sense,
But trust Him for His grace;
Behind a frowning providence
He hides a smiling face.

Providence. What a mysterious, perplexing, sometimes frustrating concept. What often appears as tragedy, emerges as triumph. What often appears as a major loss, becomes a life-changing transition. Often, that which looks hopeless, rises from the ashes as a renewed, hope-filled phoenix. What often appears as the frown of God, is merely a hidden smile.

Not even close to experiencing the same extremes of life as Cowper, I too have found that God does indeed have a smiling face, a face that is sometimes hidden behind a frown. That, for me, has proven to be part of the allurement of faith. Some of us have found that it is often beyond the frown of God that His smile is discovered.

Chapter 13: That Night

During my formative years on Roaring Creek, a highlight of the whole magical season of Christmas was the annual community Christmas program. One of the nicer touches to the annual program, was that the Missionary Baptist Church, with which I was joined at the hip, and the Freewill Baptist Church, about a quarter-mile down the road from the mother church from which she sprang, would alternate years for the presentation of the Christmas program. Inwardly, we were disappointed that our Freewill brethren had cut ties with us years and years before. But since the split occurred so many years in the past, it was rarely even discussed, and we were on friendly terms with them.

The Holiness church, about a quarter of a mile up the road from the Missionary Baptist Church, had only a few of their congregants taking part. The program was *always* presented on Christmas Eve. In a community of around only 300 people, with only one other community-wide seasonal or social event, it was a pretty big deal.

The younger children's part of the program consisted of Christmas songs and poems; and the older youths, sometimes along with a few adults, would stage a Christmas play. The drama often fluctuated between traditional and contemporary, but it was always oriented toward the sacred, incorporating the nativity into whatever format was utilized. One year, when I was 17, we actually wrote our own play.

It was during these tender years that yours truly made his performing arts debut. The critics—all three of them—gave me rave reviews. But I think that my mother and two grandmothers were a bit biased, so the reviews probably carried little weight.

For several consecutive Sunday afternoons, beginning sometime in early November, we would rehearse our lines, learn our cues, and project our voices. Our drama instructors would always try to instill the fear of God in us by saying, "Now boys and girls, on *that night* you're going to have to speak up… on *that night* you need to have your part memorized, because this building will be filled with people." One of the directors in particular just had this certain look that commanded respect. Then again, maybe she was just plain scary. She definitely had my undivided attention.

The expression, *That Night,* had an ominous ring to it, especially since the directors emphasized it through serious-looking pursed lips, along with penetrating glares. The intended purpose for their using the phrase—*That Night*—didn't bother me too much, because I've always worked better under pressure. Even as a squeaky-voiced seven-year-old, missing my two front teeth, my vocal projection surely would have made even John Chrysostom proud.

Finally, the big night of December 24—*That Night,* mind you—came. It came the same way every year. It is one of the few close encounters with anything even approximating magic that I've ever known. One of my favorite rituals in preparation for *That Night* was rummaging through a large paper poke filled with an assortment of fuzzy "beards," and selecting just the right one. Some of them were jet black, some auburn, and some sandy blond. They were made from the fur collars that had been donated from ladies' dress coats.

The girls would be fitted in their angelic robes, made of discarded white sheets. Their cardboard wings were wrapped in aluminum foil. Their halos were constructed from wire clothes hangers, then graced with gold and silver garland. It was a magical moment, seeing all the Christmas paraphernalia just magically appearing out of some mysterious hideaway, whose whereabouts were known only to the keepers of such hallowed secrets, secrets reserved only for *That Night.*

Having selected just the right beard, we shepherds and wise men attached them around our well-groomed, short-haired heads with elastic bands (not sure where the elastic came from, but the lacy white bands looked suspiciously familiar). Then, of course, there was a colorful assortment of bathrobes and towels, tall crooked staffs for the shepherds, and cardboard crowns with glistening gold and silver glitter for the three Wise Men from the East.

One geographical anomaly that always puzzled me about the Wise Men, was that I never could figure out where *Orient Are* was located. At least that's where the hymn, *We Three Kings,* said that the magi came from. But I digress. *That Night* was once again charged with sacred electricity.

Stepping from behind blue curtains, suspended by a wire attached to two eyehooks, about eight feet high, we were ready. As always, the program was a hit. The little young'uns would make their parents and grandparents beam with pride, and the older ones always seemed to get their lines just right, and if they didn't, nobody noticed or cared anyway. *That Night* was special once again, just like it had been every year before. *That Night* the directors could breathe a sigh of relief, then return to being just ordinary citizens for the next eleven months.

The grand finale of the annual program was the exchanging of the gifts displayed under the tall Christmas tree at the front of the church. To ensure that every boy and girl received a gift, we always drew names about a month before the big night. For integrity's sake, I must confess that my part of the "random" process was rigged. I know it's the equivalent of learning that *rasslin's* not real, but it's true. My fourth cousin, David Burleson, and I always made sure that we got each other's name. I know that what he and I did was as crooked as a barrel of fishhooks, but we just had to do it. Plus, we always got each other the same gifts—model cars.

The gifts were distributed by none other than Santa Claus himself, aka *Santy*. Rumor had it that Santa was really one of our less inhibited local residents, but I personally was never convinced that he was anyone other than the sainted elf himself. Being a person of keen observation, I must admit, however, that I did find it a bit suspicious that every year Santa would say something to the effect that he broke a sled runner coming across Cranberry Gap. Stranger things *have* happened, however, and I dismissed it as sheer coincidence. After all, the old-timers would have said that they don't make sled runners like they used to.

If it weren't strange enough that Santy always said something about breaking a sled runner, at one of the Christmas Eve programs, my older first cousin, Terry, stuck a hat pin in Santa's belly. It popped like a cap buster gun. My cousin thought it was funny, but some of the parents, still trying to perpetuate a little North Pole mythology, did not. Santa made a remarkable recovery, and the show went on as planned.

After the annual Christmas program, the festivities shifted gears. Having surrendered our beards, robes, staffs, and other pageant accoutrements back to the safe keeping of the hands who knew the secret storage place, it was time to breathe a sigh of relief, and look forward to another year. It wasn't just relief though, it was tainted with a touch of sadness, but we were young, and didn't give it too much thought. All that planning, all that practice, all that adrenaline, and, just like that, it was over.

With an exchanged gift in hand, it was toward the door of the packed, stuffy little church, where we were given a small, paper treat bag filled with oranges, apples, and candy. As the double doors opened, we were greeted by the biting December cold, and shocked back to reality. The drama was over, it was December 24, and it was cold. It was time to head back home, up the steep winding road that meandered through the valley and crossed two creeks, leading us to our humble haven, beneath the watchful gaze of Grassy Ridge and Big Yellow.

In preparation for the events of Christmas Eve, my mother always baked a store-bought smoked ham. The company that produced the ham featured an animated pig marching band on its TV commercials. How could we not buy ham advertised by happy, musical swine? We'd have ham sandwiches with lettuce, tomato, and mayo, between two slices of white bread. There'd be chips or potato salad, maybe some baked beans, cookies, and candy. Afterwards, we'd gather for the exchanging of gifts in our small, plainly furnished living room.

In my family, a tradition gradually developed over the years in which we opened gifts on Christmas Eve rather than on Christmas morning. My mother insisted that its basis was theological in part, because most of the momentous events surrounding the birth of the Christ child occurred at night, not during broad daylight. Hmm, good point!

Before settling down for the night before Christmas, there was one more item of business on the agenda for the young and the young at heart—*farcrackers*. I'd usually get together with cousins, who in all honesty could have included virtually anyone on the creek, and we'd fire off our pyrotechnics, either beside the road or in a big field up above my house. Even though the possession and discharge of fireworks was illegal in North Carolina, the way I saw it, it was for a good cause. (1) We were tickled to death that Christ was born, and wanted to do our part to remind everybody; and (2) in purchasing our illegal wares, we had made significant contributions to the economy of Carter County, Tennessee, our friendly neighbor to the West. It was a goodwill gesture from any angle you considered it.

Everyone knows about the warning label on fireworks: *Light fuse and get away.* We took that to mean, "When I light this fuse, you'd better get away from me, 'cause I'm gonna shoot it at you!" We actually had friendly fights with bottle rockets and Roman candles. "Careful! You could put an eye out!!!" suddenly made sense. By the grace of God, I never made the acquaintance of a single one-eyed kid, nor did I become one. But our parents insisted that they were out there. For quite a number of years, I was an excellent potential candidate.

With the grime and scent of gunpowder on our hands and clothes, and a few holes melted into our nylon jackets, we'd part company, going our separate ways to our own homes. I'd come in out of the cold and have another sandwich, and warm by the wood stove. The excitement would wind down, the remaining shreds of wrapping paper, boxes, bows, and ribbons would be cleared away, and it was time for bed.

My thoughts and prayers would trail off with something like "Got exactly what I wanted this year... hope they like what I got them... can't wait to try that race track set and BB gun out tomorrow... boy I'm glad school's out... I love farworks... we done good in that play tonight... thank you Lord, for sending Jesus, and... zzzzzzzzzzz."

The next day, Christmas day, we'd visit and exchange gifts with both sets of my grandparents. Donning new shirts, pants, skirts, or sweaters, we'd gather together around the table, usually at my house, for a sumptuous feast of turkey and ham, mashed potatoes, gravy, turkey dressing, green beans, rolls, cranberry sauce, and enough dessert to bewilder even the heartiest pancreas. My mother would snap the inevitable "feast photo," depicting the House of Hughes in their natural habitat, doing what they did better than anything else.

Slowly, almost imperceptibly at first, our Christmas celebrations on the Creek assumed a new look. When you're young, carefree, and more ignorant than when you're older, you think it'll never end. You assume that nothing will ever change, that the predicable sameness will always be there. What blissful ignorance! And it really is blissful, because young children probably *ought* to think that way.

As we grew older, some of us moved farther away, and our own families began to take center stage. The winding road through the valley is paved now, and the annual Christmas program started occurring on nights other than December 24th. I'm not sure if the two churches still host it on alternate years. Our local Santa doesn't stop by for his visit anymore, and there aren't many fireworks now.

Despite the changes, just like always, Christmas still comes. It will come again and again. It's different, but it is as unstoppable as the wind. The Spirit of Christmas defies all attempts at eradication, modernization, and complication. It came nearly two thousand times before I was here, and its faithful herald will blast the silent night and shatter the slumber of human despair long after I'm gone.

If I could turn back the immovable hands of time, would I? Yes, I probably would, but only temporarily. Even if I could, I shouldn't, because I've learned that Christmas is vastly larger than me and the goings on in my little world. No change can alter it. No sorrow can drown it. No adversity can tarnish it. The gentle roar of the message of the manger still echoes down the corridors of my soul, and rings from the sides of the valley which I call home.

Whether it's Christmas on the Creek, or Christmas in the big city, or Christmas in the tropics, that's the *soul* of Christmas, the *inner sanctum*, the *holy of holies.* And *that* is the elusive, gloriously mysterious part that the wrinkled hand of time shall never touch, nor seize, nor overcome.

Chapter 14: That Ol' Broke Down Gyarden Gate

"I can jes' see that ol' broke down gyarden gate."

A published friend of mine suggested that I use one of my sermons in my book. I decided to incorporate my maternal grandmother's eulogy, which I delivered on April 13, 2000. Strictly speaking, a sermon is not the same as a eulogy, so this is the closest that I will venture to that.

I'm not sure what it says about me, but within my tiny circle, I have a good reputation for my eulogies and memorials. Maybe part of the reason is because they are usually brief and to the point, and I've never been criticized either for a short sermon or a short eulogy.

I don't know if or how well my incorporation of a eulogy will go over, so it was a definite roll of the dice. Let me elucidate my rationale. In a direct and personal way, perhaps no one whose name I've included in this book epitomizes the first twenty years of my life more so than Grandma Hazel. I was *not* closer to her than to my own my mother, but I spent a lot of time at her house in my formative years. Also, with her having been born in 1911, her life simply encompassed an enormous amount of epochal transition. Grandma Hazel's passing was, for me at least, far more than the departure of a grandparent, it represented the passing of an era.

In my four-plus decades' worth of ministerial experience, I have presided over literally hundreds of memorial services, whether in a church sanctuary, a funeral home chapel, a private home setting, or a graveside. Out of all the *good words* (literal meaning of *eulogy*) that I have spoken over family, friends, and acquaintances, there are four instances that, in my estimation, stand head and shoulders above the rest. Listed in chronological

129

order, those four eulogies are: Grandma Hazel's, my father's, a co-worker/friend's, and my mother's.

Grandma Hazel suffered a terrible stroke not very long after Grandpas Jack passed in 1994. She lived out her remaining days in a nursing home, before passing at a local hospital in April 2000, at 88 years of age.

Eulogy for Grandma Hazel
Roaring Creek Missionary Baptist Church
April 13, 2000
by
Rev. Chris R. Hughes

"Whenever I walk or drive past a dilapidated old house or a tottering, decaying barn, groaning under the merciless weight of time and change, I always experience feelings of bittersweetness. Once those old houses and barns were young and strong, now they're old and falling down. Still, they stand as reminders of better days past.

"Old houses and barns have a story to tell. If they could invite us to sit a spell in a creaking rocking chair on a rickety front porch, or curl up on a pile of musty hay, what we would hear! They could tell us about the good times, the sad times, the days of lean, and those of plenty. We'd cry, we'd laugh, but mostly we would listen with purpose.

"Oftentimes, these crumbling skeletons are surrounded by sagging fences, which have surrendered to an advancing army of weeds, briars, and vines, not to mention gravity itself. There'll be a point where the fence yields way to a gate, or, in some cases, where a gate used to be.

"These old gates all seem to wear the same expressions. The rusted hinges, if connected at all, are pulling away from the posts, drawn by an irresistible force. The gate will be tilted toward the earth like an ancient warrior with his head bowed in bitter defeat, never fully conceding victory to a younger, stronger opponent than he. These old gates are tougher than they look. Sometimes they never do fall, they just rot and vanish into oblivion, leaving only a piece or two of hardware to remind us that they ever existed at all.

"Not too terribly long ago, before the hourglass had emptied its final grains of sand, Grandma Hazel lived in a tottering old house, surrounded by a sagging fence with four wooden gates. Like an old farmer with a walking cane, a sway-backed barn shakily stood just above the house. The smokehouse out behind the house had long since served its purpose. The frog pond had been invaded with saplings, briars, and weeds. Altering everything it touches, time had made a change, and would continue its tireless circuit.

"On one of her scores of missions of mercy to see her own mother, my mother listened helplessly and sadly as Grandma Hazel talked about the old home place. Despite the depleted storehouse of memory, there were scenes, people, and events that still shone brightly in her declining memory. Her left arm was withered and twisted like the weather-beaten branches of the oak trees on the lower side of the Big Yellow. In a faraway, quivering voice, laden with nostalgia, she talked about her longing to go back home. In her unmistakable brogue, inherited from her vigorous Scot-Irish ancestors, she said, 'I jes' 'onta go home. I can jes' see that ol' broke down gyarden gate.'

"Etched so deeply upon her mind, the image of that old broke down garden gate was so powerful that you could almost smell the musty scent of rotting pine. It seemed you could see what little was left of the peeling white paint, and hear the creaking of rusty hinges, whose holes were already crowded with extra nails in an attempt to stave off the relentless pull of gravity.

"A little over three years before she passed, close to Christmastime, I got the notion to take my 8mm camcorder into room 108 at the Brian Center Nursing facility in Spruce Pine, and record Grandma as we shared a good visit. I positioned the camera on a tripod so as not to make it so obvious that I was recording our conversation. Grandma didn't know much about camcorders, but then again, neither did I, so we made a good pair. It was a bit slow and awkward at first, but after I got Grandma going, the conversation flowed as smoothly as the Elk Holler Creek on a late September afternoon, whisking away the leaves of yet another summer.

"Grandma and I had a good visit that day in the nursing home. I can't answer for her, but for me at least, it was a very special moment, one which I considered sacred. Of course, given her condition, she said a few things that were not exactly on the level, but that day, as well as almost every other time I visited Grandma, she knew me, and talked to me. It is a deeply humbling experience to speak to someone whose only remaining faculty is their distant memory. In that manner, you learn a lot about what has been important to people.

"On that December afternoon, I realized something about Grandma Hazel that had mostly evaded my attention throughout my entire life. It was this: Grandma Hazel had lived virtually all of her life largely unaware of the times. I figured that by her marrying and having her first child when she was just 15, nothing unusual for her generation, and doing whatever she had to do just to survive, she had a pretty good excuse not to get too preoccupied with the shifting landscape of time. She'd been kept plenty busy just trying to keep her footing.

"Having been around Grandma Hazel from the time I was a chubby baby, I doubt if she even knew the price of light bread and shoes, much less what was happening in the rapidly changing sphere of world events or technology. But if you asked her about comforting a broken-hearted child, how to cook a pot of October beans, the signs of the moon, or the medicinal value of snuff spit, she was in her element.

"This time-warp in which Grandma lived, really had little or nothing to do with intelligence, but it had nearly everything to do with priorities. Life becomes a matter of what one thinks is most important. The price of light bread and shoes, and world news were just not terribly important to Grandma. To her, those were other people's concerns.

"Just like these old broke down garden gates, there aren't all that many things that are of great consequence. Garden gates are concerned only with letting things in that ought to be let in, and keeping things out that don't belong. That's kind of like what Grandma did.

"I can't really say if Grandma Hazel knew that Christmas was only about a week away, or if she knew the names of her nurses, or how much aware she was of her surroundings. When I managed to steer the conversation back across the paths and backroads of memory, however, she waxed so eloquently. She spoke with crystal clarity about people and events that were then only faded memories.

"With the camcorder battery fading fast, we moved as swiftly as the fog across the Roan Ridge. We flew back across the ages—sixty, seventy, even eighty years. For a few moments, I felt as if Grandma had motioned for me to slip behind the curtain of time, and skip with her across the fragrant meadows, as if we were two carefree children. For the next thirty minutes or so, she served as my seasoned tour guide, pointing out what for me were scenes that were strangely fascinating. It was one of those moments when Father Time slowed his gait to give us just a few more fleeting moments. As if I had been swept away to a once-upon-a-time-land, I was allowed to travel back to an era when the garden gate still bore the pleasant scent and proud look of fresh, white paint.

"The sights, sounds, and colors of the past came alive that day. She talked of Delphie Edards (Edwards), Charlie Thomas, and Mother Ebb (her mother). As she described them, I could just see some of those legendary old-timers. I've either only heard of or barely remember most of them. I visualized them meandering their way down muddy paths off the ridges. Their hands were stained by the black dirt from a new ground. I could see mothers carrying whimpering young'uns wrapped in tattered blankets. She told me how she and Grandpa Jack used to walk with my mother on her hip down to Jeffie Hughes' store. She talked about those old-timey, red-hot, pew-jumping, revival meetings, way back in the day.

"Life was mostly hard for Grandma Hazel. The mural of her life had been painted with a lot of dark hues. There were the deep blue shades of depression, the grays of uncertainty, the indigos of utter sadness, the crimsons of deepest hurt. To be sure, there were a few yellows of laughter, some violets of happiness, and some greens of hope.

"All who knew her would surely agree that Grandma had her own way of describing things. As if it were yesterday, I can still hear her say, 'That smells plime blank like ol' cyarn!' For the sake of the uninitiated, the translation of that expression is, 'That smells exactly like rotten flesh.'

"More than once, I remember dashing into her kitchen as a skinny, freckled-faced, cabbage-eared boy, and going over to the stove and wolfing down spoonfuls of cold, stewed potatoes. Grandma looked on with some disgust saying, 'Why Chris, they ain't nothin' no sorrier than old cold taters!' But to me, they tasted like a gourmet dish. Oh, for another bowl of her cold, stewed potatoes!

"Even when I deserved it, which honestly was pretty often, Grandma was reluctant to dish out punishment. Even though I spent a good bit of my childhood under Grandma Hazel's tutelage, I don't think she ever gave me a spanking. She did, however, threaten me with the possibility of being put in a tow sack and carried off to hell by a pitch fork-toting Satan, to whom she grimly referred as the *Ol' Sack Naz*. I would have preferred a spanking. I never have completely figured out the origin or logic of that expression, *Ol' Sack Naz*. Just the very sound of the words, *'Ol' Sack Naz,'* coming from my bespectacled Grandma's wrinkled mouth, with dried snuff in the corners, was enough to frighten me into good behavior for at least five minutes.

"She really got to me one time. I guess you could say she scared the hell out of me. I asked her if the devil was really going to come and get me and put me in his tow sack. She said something like, 'No, he ain't a gonna git ye! Yore s' mean he wouldn't have ye!' In a strange sort of way, I found temporary comfort in those words, however frightening. *Ol' Sack Naz* and all, life was so full of carefree living...before the garden gate broke down.

"Like many who had gone before her, Grandma knelt at life's spring and drank deeply, sometimes finding the waters to be bitter. In June of 1994, she lost her life's companion of 68 years, Grandpa Jack. He had been a caring and solid mate for Grandma. It seems that after he went on, the old garden gate really broke down.

"The more I've thought about it the more I've come to realize that, like Grandma Hazel, we all just want to go home in one way or another. We grow up, we get preoccupied, changes come in various shapes, sizes and degrees, and before we know it, time has left its mark and taken its inevitable toll.

"Maybe you've never thought of it this way, but in some ways, the Bible is a story of three gardens. The ancient story of redemption opens in Genesis. Before very long, we find ourselves in a beautiful garden, surrounded by every good thing imaginable. Seemingly, that didn't last long. Our first parents didn't keep God's commandment, and were driven out of paradise. The gate to Eden was slammed shut and guarded by mighty cherubim, bearing flaming swords. We've been traveling east of Eden ever since. We know there's a God-shaped hole in the deepest, most sacred part of our being, and nothing we put in it seems to fit. We have a longing for a home we've never seen, a love we've never experienced, a relationship we've never fully embraced. But the gate was closed.

"In His great mercy and love for our fallen race, God came to earth as a baby boy. He faced everything that we face, experienced everything we experience, but with one exception: He was without sin. He was baptized in the Jordan river, tempted by the devil, transfigured on the mountain, healed the sick, cleansed the lepers, opened the eyes of the blind, and even raised the dead.

"One night, when Jesus was about 33 years old, he walked into a garden and prayed in the shadow of huge, ancient olive trees in the garden of Gethsemane. He was arrested, was given a mockery of a trial, and was crucified between two thieves on Golgotha. A rich man took his body and laid it in a garden tomb. Three days later He rose from the dead. Forty days after that, He went back to heaven. Now, according to a vision that John the revelator had, Jesus Christ, the eternal Son of God, owns the keys of death, and the underworld. He's the real gatekeeper, He's got the keys!

"Finally, the story of the Bible closes in a garden. This garden is unlike anything in this present world. In Revelation

21 and 22, John describes this garden as a place where everything bad has passed away, a place where there's no such thing as night, pain, sickness, tears, sin, and death. He describes it as a place with a crystal-clear river, a fruit tree bearing twelve kinds of fruit, and a place of total peace and joy. He also said that this place is surrounded by twelve gates. Each gate is made of a single pearl, they're never closed, and they won't ever break down and fall off the hinges.

"A few months before she passed, I visited Grandma Hazel in the hospital. The thought occurred to me that I ought to ask Grandma, if for no other reason than to soothe my own conscience, if she was ready to meet her Lord. I knew she was, but I just wanted to hear her say it, rather than my assuming it. I said, 'Grandma, when the Lord sends after you, are you ready to meet Him?' In the strongest voice I had heard her use since before her first stroke, she looked me square in the eye and said, 'Yes sir!' I did not deserve being called 'Sir' by my own grandmother, but it simply gave her confession a ring of authority. I believed her then as now. I had no doubt then as well now that she was ready to meet the Lord.

"I'm looking forward to seeing Grandma Hazel again. I say that with confidence. In the hope of a blessed resurrection, we'll embrace once again by one of God's garden gates."

....

The very next morning, after the night of Grandma Hazel's memorial service, we went to Hughes Cemetery, aka the Upper Cemetery, on Jerry's Creek for her graveside service and burial. Jeremiah Hughes, the first white settler of Roaring Creek, rests in peace in that same cemetery.

My part of that service, as is overwhelmingly the case while officiating at gravesides, was traditional, brief, and routine. At the very end of the service, I did something that was anything but traditional and routine, but something that I felt to be very appropriate.

The night before, during the memorial service, I told my Minneapolis Elementary bean story, the same as I included earlier in the chapter about soup beans. At the graveside, I read Psalm 1. Part of Psalm 1 compares wicked people to chaff, in stark contrast to righteous people, who are compared to sturdy trees. Once as a small boy, I watched Grandma Hazel winnow out the chaff from a double-handful of dried beans. As Grandma worked her magic, the chaff was borne away on the determined but gentle wings of the Northwest wind. The only thing left after the winnowing was a beautiful portion of dried beans.

In my sphere, it is customary at the very conclusion of a graveside service for the minister and pall bearers to remove their boutonnieres and place them at the head of the casket. After placing my boutonniere on the casket, I reached in the right-hand side pocket of my suit coat, and pulled out a plain white handkerchief, with a handful of beans wrapped in it. I placed it, alongside my boutonniere, at the head of the casket. I cannot think of more appropriate, reverential manner in which I could have honored my grandmother.

An era had passed. That ol' broke down 'gyarden' gate finally gave out. Unabated, time marched on.

Chapter 15: All Work and No Play?

Don't think for a moment that all of my family's life on the Creek was work, work, and more work. Most of it was, but we knew how to have some occasional fun too. If fun were the constant norm, it would lose its sparkle. But fun paints life with accents of bright colors, and punctuates the hum drum with exclamation points.

We didn't really do family vacations, and didn't normally travel very far from home. Every once in a great while, we'd go to Valdese, North Carolina to visit Grandpa Rob's family, and a couple of times, went to Wilmington to visit Pam. Even still, I didn't feel deprived, and was always glad to get back to home sweet home.

Some of the activities that I deemed fun would not be so enjoyable to most people. But we all experience life and its passing moments differently. It's all a matter of perspective. For example, I'm guessing that working long hours in a hay field is not most people's idea of R & R. I feel exactly the same way whenever I drive past a golf course or tennis court. I have neither the interest in nor the desire for either golf or tennis.

I currently live about fifteen miles from one of the major NASCAR venues. No reflection either on that or any other stock car racing organization, but they would have to pay *me* to go to one of those races! Fellow Highlanders and friends in general, please forgive me if the idea of sitting amongst 100,000 or so people, watching really loud, really fast cars go round and round doesn't appeal to me, but so be it. I like drag racing, particularly funny cars and top fuelers, but not stock car racing. I simply lack the attention span. And I just happen to prefer the exponentially more powerful top fuelers and funny cars.

I'll go ahead and knock out what may seem like some oddball things that I remember as fun. I'll start with fence-building. I loved going out to the locust patch with daddy, watching him fall a huge yellow locust with laser precision with his trusty chainsaw, then cutting it up into six-foot lengths. He would painstakingly use a sledge hammer and several wedges to split fence posts out of those lengths. He would sharpen one end of the posts like a hypodermic needle. I'd help of course, but he did most of the hard stuff.

We would then carry the posts to the area of pasture or lot where they would be strategically placed. Daddy would start a small hole with a heavy crowbar, then drive the posts in the ground about a foot deep with a sledgehammer. We would then roll out either woven wire or barbwire, and secure it to the posts. I particularly liked using the wire stretcher to make the fencing taut.

Another *different* kind of fun was actually one of the highlights of my entire year—putting up hay with Grandpa Jack. I loved putting up hay any chance I got, but Grandpa Jack had several big meadows of hay, and naturally, it took much longer. We put up hay only once a year, always in August, as I recall.

The Trivette brothers and Monroe Thomas, from Gouge's Creek, near the Mitchell County line, were the first ones who were hired to do the motorized cutting, raking, and baling. I remember their three tractors—two David Brown's and an ancient Ford. Later, in the early 70's, it was Homer Hicks and his two boys, who used an International and a Case tractor. Before the Trivettes and Hicks', the men stacked hay vertically with pitchforks on nice, neat shock poles.

I loved everything about putting up hay. To this day there are few fragrances that I cherish more than a freshly mown meadow. Once the hay was baled in those square bales that you rarely see these days, it was time to load 'em up and move 'em out. We'd assemble a convoy of maybe two or three trucks—pick-up trucks or larger trucks—and toss those bales into the beds of the trucks. One person would stack, while the rest of us followed the trucks and tossed up the bales.

After a truck was loaded to capacity, it was time to head to the barn, just a little less than a half mile away. Once we got to the barn, it was the same process in reverse, except there'd be at least a couple of people in the barn loft to help carry and stack the bales. It could get really interesting if there happened to be a nest or two of wasps or bumblebees that had staked claims on the barn loft! At the end of the long day, Grandpa Jack would always hand me a $5.00 bill.

Not only did hay time come in August, so did the traveling carnival. Every year, one of those little rinky-dink traveling carnivals would set up shop in the county seat of Newland. That $5.00 hay money went pretty far, but wasn't long for this world when the carnival came. The Newland carnival was my equivalent of going to a theme park. I loved those gut-wrenching carnival rides; the scent of popcorn, peanuts, and a dozen other goodies; cotton candy all over my face; and a newly acquired taste for vinegar on French fries.

While I'm on an August roll, I may as well mention Decoration Day. After I explain what Decoration Day is, this will be another one of those things that will leave you wondering "What was fun about *that*?" Decoration Day is a custom that is practiced in several parts of the Southern Appalachians, and, so I've been told, in a few other places as well. People gather in a cemetery and place flowers on the graves of departed loved ones to honor their memory. On Roaring Creek, Decoration Day always occurs on the first two Sundays in August. By that time, the dahlias (sometimes called tater roses), gladiolus, and some other flowers are in full bloom.

At my home place there's a hydrangea tree, actually one of the two largest ones I've ever seen, that produces huge, football-size pinkish/white blooms that became a fixture at Decoration Day.

The reason Decoration Day took two Sundays is because there are two public cemeteries on Roaring Creek. Both are located on Jerry's Creek. We knew them simply as the Lower Cemetery and the Upper Cemetery due their relative altitude in relation to Jerry's Creek. Lower Cemetery is nearly full, but there's still room to spare at the Upper (actually named Hughes) Cemetery.

On each of the two Decoration Day Sundays, an open-air church service was held. Whomever was pastor at the Freewill Baptist Church preached on one of the Decoration Days, and the pastor from the Missionary Baptist Church preached the remaining Sunday. Folks from both churches provided some singing. I'm not really certain if this same protocol is followed these days, but that's how was done in the days of yore.

The simple reason that I included Decoration Day as a "fun event" is because it was one of only a thimble-full of community events that was held on the Creek. It was a major social gathering that strengthened the ties that bound. Auld acquaintances would be renewed, our kin would come from beyond the immediate area, and hugs and handshakes were aplenty. If all that wasn't enough, when the festivities were over, my family would gather with some extended family at one of my grandparents' homes, or my home, and have a feast befitting the Roman Senate.

My version of demolition derby was rolling rocks. By rolling rocks, I mean going up on the side of a steep hill, finding and dislodging the biggest, roundest rocks possible, and getting them started on a furious roll down that hill. Oh man! That's a lot of force, especially with those big rocks! They wouldn't get too far before colliding with a tree. Sometimes I could see it happen, most of the times I'd just hear a violent thud somewhere way down below.

Rolling rocks in the summer of '78, I got pinned under a big granite rock. I almost qualified for one of the Darwin Awards. My fourth cousin, David Hughes, and I were just a few yards above Clay Calhoun's. We happened upon one fine rock, just begging to be let loose down an embankment. I didn't want this perfect wrecking ball of a rock to tear Clay's fence down, and I'm pretty sure he wouldn't have wanted that either. So, I had what I thought was a brilliant engineering idea, apparently borrowed from the slapstick comedy playbook.

About three years older than David, I was considerably bigger and stronger than he. The plan was for David to push the rock toward me, with me being positioned on a slight downhill angle from the rock. According to plan, after David pushed the rock toward me, I would roll it diagonally to the left of Clay's fence. It was a brilliant strategy…I thought. I gave the word, "Go ahead, push it toward me, I've got it!" Rarely have my words been more prophetic. I *got it* alright. That rock was *way* heavier than I thought, and I didn't roll it anywhere. It slowly, irresistibly pushed me to the ground, even separating the thick denim fabric of my blue jeans in my inner quadricep area. Frankengranite pinned my right hand and both legs. I was flat of my back facing downhill, and couldn't persuade that rock to release me. No amount of wiggling, pushing, or straining even fazed that oblivious rock. David was too small and weak, and he couldn't budge it. He had the good sense to go get Nell and Ivette Hicks, and they lifted it just enough for me to get out from under it.

Somewhere in the all the commotion, my parents found out about my momentous rock n' roll adventure, and showed up at the scene. They were pretty rattled. Daddy's words of comfort consisted of, "You had no business up here to start with!" I guess some folks just have a peculiar way of showing alarm and concern.

To this day, cousin Phillip, David's older brother, calls me *Avalanche*. I don't recommend getting a new nickname in that manner. I also have a better understanding as to why women outlive men.

Before anyone ever heard of bungee jumping, there was an outrageously fun sport known to all of us little ridge runners—swinging on grapevines. All of the vines weren't actual grapevines, but they looked exactly like grapevines. These strong, cable-like vines would wrap themselves around tall trees, and just keep climbing. Finding a long, thick vine in a massive, stately poplar tree was a real treasure. Tarzan, Lord of the Apes had nothing on Chris, Lord of the frog pond. We'd grab hold of the bottom end of the vine, back ourselves up a hill or embankment as far as possible, and hold on for dear life.

The topmost tendrils of those vines are not all that strong. Trust me, I know this to be a fact. I had one of those vines to break with me one time, just as I swung way out over the creek, having been launched from a high, steep embankment. With the back of my head coming down hard on a rock, it was pretty scary, but I wasn't nearly as upset about it as my good friend T.W. Hopson. I could almost cry, forty-something years after the fact, over how upset T.W. was. He thought I was hurt badly. He was right to think that.

Given the height of that vine, the trajectory of the swinging movement, the momentum, force, and angle with which I hit that rock, I *should have been* hurt badly or worse. But I wasn't. Or maybe I was and just didn't know it at the time. If so, it sure would help to explain some things. It was roughly the equivalent of that predictable precursor to disaster, "Hey ya'll, watch this!"

One of the most anticipated fun things I did was camping out, usually on a warm-enough Friday night. My earliest camping trips involved no tents, just open-air sleeping in a sleeping bag, and being covered with cold dew upon waking. Usually, I camped with two or three buddies, and never ventured more than a few miles from home. By my mid-teens, we all had motorcycles, and naturally, went a bit further.

Between eighth grade and my freshman year of high school, three of my friends and I embarked on a three-day/three-night adventure, on foot. Night one was spent on Big Yellow Mountain. It rained. Night two was at the Low Gap, between Yellow Mountain Gap and Grassy Ridge Bald. It rained. On night three, we finally caught a break from the rain on Grassy Ridge Bald. In three days/nights, the four of us went through a whole carton of chewing tobacco. A carton consisted of twelve pouches, equaling three pouches each.

The morning after Grassy Ridge, we carefully made our way over a boulder field on the south-facing end of Grassy Ridge. We finally ended up on a beautiful ridge called Cherry Orchard, then past the Stuart house, and eventually down Jerry's Creek. Priceless memories.

As a youngster, I didn't really enjoy working in the garden. Actually, I hated it. However, garden work wasn't a suggestion, and there was no option clause. It would be many years in the future before I would both appreciate and enjoy it. From a very young age, I had to help plant the vegetables, cultivate the vegetables, harvest the vegetables. Damned vegetables! But now, I'm so glad that it wasn't optional.

On occasion, after a morning of slaving amongst the vegetables, namely corn and potatoes, under the stern eye of Jarge the Taskmaster, he would say "J'u 'onna go t' river?" Translation: "Do you want to go to the river?" Did I want to go to the river? That'd be like asking a rooster if he wanted to go to a redworm convention! Of course, I wanted to go to the river! That meant that I got to go fishing in Toe River, just under three miles away, with my daddy. I loved going to Toe River with him. I think it was his consolation prize to me for working in the vegetable patch in the summer sun.

When we went to the river, that meant two things among others: (1) there was much more variety in the possibility of the catch—maybe trout, maybe bluegills, maybe red eyes, maybe a big, slimy hellbender/waterdog; (2) there was a far greater likelihood of catching a large trout. Those five simple words, "J'u 'onna go t' river?" or eight if you spell them out completely, were some of the most cherished words I ever heard. I never caught anything big, but I got to go t' river with daddy. That was good enough.

Warning: not everything that I deemed to be fun would be safe or sensible, but I did it anyway. I am part of the reason that TV entertainment shows sometimes warn their audience: "Do Not Try This at Home."

Some people think that the insulation has come off of my wiring because I absolutely love snow. Oddly enough, lots of people back home don't care for snow at all. My question to them is, "Why live in the mountains?" I love those big, heavy, deep snows that we used get when the seasons were reliably predictable. I enjoy the anticipation of a big snow almost as much as the snow itself. Long before the snow begins to fall, you can feel it and smell it in the very air.

Part of the reason for my love of snow is because some of the greatest fun I ever had was being out of school and playing in the snow. Just being out of school was great fun in and of itself, but playing in a frozen white wonderland was even better.

In the winter of 1977-1978, I was in the eleventh grade. Starting the second week of January of '78, Avery County schools were closed forty-one days in a row! I cherished every second.

After a good snow, good enough to cover the gravel roads thoroughly, making driving difficult, the snow sleds were readied. If enough vehicular travel had established some good routes in the snow, and one of the county snow plows had further compacted the snowy roads, the winter games would begin. We would pull our sleds up the road past S.D. and Verna Beam's place. Sometimes we'd sled on Jerry's Creek, which has an even longer, steeper incline than the main road where I lived.

We'd get those sleds going as fast as possible on the gleaming, slick roads. We'd race, try to wreck each other, and even ride at night. Night was even better, because we could see vehicles coming. Besides that, when those steel runners contacted gravel, sparks would fly. Sometimes during those night adventures, we'd a build a small fire and roast potatoes in the coals. It is a testament to Providence that, as far as know, no one was killed or seriously injured.

Besides sledding on the roads, we'd take big truck innertubes, and even pieces of wall paneling up to one of the many cleared fields. You've never been blessed until you've ridden a piece of slick paneling, with a string tied to the front. If you didn't pull the front edge up enough with the attached string, the paneling would mire up in the snow. If you pulled up too much on the string, you'd go airborne and flip. Sometimes we'd make ramps for the innertubes and paneling, or whatever we could find that would slide in the snow. Occasionally, during those splendid days, we long-headed younguns' would ride old car hoods with four or five of us piled on.

One of the most unusual traits of my immediate family was that we rarely played music in the home, and *never* played it over the car or house radio. The radio was considered to be just another form of noise. My folks used the radio primarily for two reasons: (1) the weather forecast; (2) the daily obituaries. The one music exception in my home was *The Gospel Singing Jubilee,* that aired every Sunday morning on the TV that picked up three channels. I loved that show. There was also the *Huff Cook Show* out of Bristol, Virginia, on which my wife and her family had appeared in her childhood.

Daddy and I would sometimes watch the *Gospel Singing Jubilee* together. As Southern Gospel music goes, it was a quality program. The show would feature some of the big names at the time—the Blackwood Brothers, the Cathedral Quartet, the Happy Goodmans, the Hinson Family, the Inspirations, J.D. Sumner and the Stamps, the Kingsmen, et al. Even if Southern Gospel is not your cup of tea, those groups back in the day weren't just entertainers with big hair and gaudy outfits, they could really sing, and knew *how* to sing.

I became enamored with Southern Gospel after mommy and daddy took me to a few gospel concerts in the Avery High School gymnasium. Let me tell you something, if you had ever heard the late, great Vestal Goodman, whose original intent was to study for the Metropolitan Opera, belt out *God Walks the Dark Hills*, or the Hinsons perform *The Lighthouse,* you might've become a fan yourself.

Personally, I'm pretty eclectic when it comes to music. I like Beethoven, The Beatles, and Blues; Choral music, Chopin, and Conway Twitty; Gregorian Chant, George Gershwin, and George Jones; Progressive Bluegrass, Pop, and Patsy Cline; Soft Rock and Southern Gospel; Mozart and Motown; Opera and the Grand Old Opry.

When I was about 9, I decided to play guitar. I got myself one of those Mel Bay guitar chord books, and I'd hole up in my bedroom and play. I took lessons for a short time, but lost interest. I really cannot say that I play guitar, but I strum a little bit, just enough to be a menace to society.

I'll mention one other fun thing, the most fun thing that my immediate family did. We did cookouts. When I say we did cookouts, what that meant was that we would box up pots, pans, enough food for a pack of coyotes, and go someplace and cook over an open fire. Sometimes we'd go to the head of Roaring Creek, or maybe Big Falls in Elk Hollow. Our two favorite places away from the Creek were the Linville Falls picnic area, and Roan Mountain State Park.

My mother was at her best when we went on a cookout. She was in her element. We'd build a small fire, and cook up fatback and streaked meat, mostly for the grease, then fry potatoes, onions, chicken, groundhog, pork chops, and make boiled coffee in a large Maxwell House coffee tin can. We'd also bring along some fresh garden veggies—onions, green peppers, tomatoes, etc.

If we happened to be cooking out in Elk Hollow, we'd fry up a bunch of freshly-caught speckled trout, rolled in cornmeal. A big speckled trout might be 6 or 7 inches, and it took a slew of them to make a mess. They could be eaten bones and all. Ask me how I know. How good they were!

One item that we'd almost always fix on a cookout was a dish that I've never heard of except on Roaring Creek. We called it *Dead Man*. Just settle down now, it has nothing to do with zombies or cannibalism. The base of Dead Man is cornbread. To that base is added a generous amount of grease, not vegetable oil, but grease. Then, in no particular order, we added chopped onions, potted meat, eggs, and enough water to make it moist. The closest thing I can compare it to would be turkey dressing. Well, maybe turkey dressing laced with meth, and chased with moonshine. It is a legal dish though.

All of our cookouts weren't off premises. Daddy would sometimes fire up the charcoal grill on a Saturday afternoon. He would grill hamburgers, and maybe some hotdogs. I don't know which one of us, daddy or me, loved burgers the best. He and I would always eat a minimum of two burgers each, and sometimes three. Occasionally, we'd have several other entrée-worthy dishes like barbeque chicken or fried chicken, and invite other family members to join us.

We're told that of our five senses, our sense of smell creates the closest link with our emotions. For example, have you ever walked into a room that smells just like your deceased grandma's house used to smell? It may have been even decades since you were in her house, and it may no longer even exist. But it doesn't matter, because that link has already been established by electrical paths in your brain. It brings back a flood of emotions, doesn't it? To this day, anytime I catch a whiff of an evening campfire, or food being grilled over burning charcoal, that scent links up with such deep emotions, and conjures up such nostalgia.

My upbringing was simple, plain, and pretty barebones basic. I'm grateful for that, and feel blessed beyond measure. There's a profundity in simplicity. I attribute my love of life's free, simple things to my tender years.

I am blessed to have been nurtured in a place where the hazy peaks of the Blue Ridge Mountains kiss the face of the sky. On winter days, I've walked through a surreal world of rime ice, clinging to the limbs and twigs of the trees on the high mountains, blindingly brilliant in the high sun against the azure backdrop of the sky. With the whole outdoors as my playground, I've played endless hours in the creek till my lips turned blue, swung on wild vines, and rolled rocks down steep hillsides. I've eaten wild strawberries in the fields, black cherries picked right off the tree, and wild peppermint growing beside tiny streams. I've heard thunderstorms rumbling out of the Northwest, watched deep snows move in from the South, and listened to the Eastern wind roar across the summit of the Big Butte like a freight train. I grew up in a time and a place in which I had two parents, enjoyed four seasons, and ate three square meals a day. I am *profoundly* grateful.

Sleeping blissfully through the night, in the mountain oat grass on Big Yellow Mountain, then being greeted by the friendly morning sun as it pops open an eyelid from the rolling Piedmont, doesn't cost a thing. I've never been charged an admission price for sitting on the front porch during a ferocious thunderstorm, while enjoying every window-rattling peal of thunder rumbling down the valley. There was no monthly charge for listening to the white noise lullaby of the creek as it wafted through my bedroom window at night. Playing with harmless old June bugs; feeding nightcrawlers to my pet toad Herman; catching lightning bugs then putting them in a mayonnaise jar with air holes poked in the lid, then bringing them into my room at night; discovering, but having the sense not to touch a nest of baby birds; skipping rocks in the creek; taking the time to smell the lilacs and peonies; looking with awe on God's palette of Fall colors; listening to the piercing cry of the red-tailed hawk; hearing the haunting "hoot, hoot" of the great horned owl; and watching the western sun slip behind the lovely veil of the Roan Ridge—all so profoundly simple, all so simply profound, all so utterly priceless.

Chapter 16: Way Up Yonder

It might have been just as appropriate for me to have included this chapter in the one about the geography of Place, or the one on what we did for fun, or even the one on religion. I'm not a pantheist or an animist, but while being in the great outdoors, especially on a mountaintop, I've always felt closer to the Creator. Considering how very much I love the Roan Highlands, I decided that my beloved peaks deserved their very own chapter.

I vividly remember being a preteen boy, staring up at Grassy Ridge Bald, our guardian to the West. Grassy Ridge is only slightly lower in elevation than Roan High Knob. I could make out the dark green of the balsam trees, and patches of yellow-green oat grass. Not far from the mouth of Roaring Creek, you're staring up at Grassy Ridge as it stares back with a comforting but no-nonsense gaze, like a 6500-foot pyramid-shaped giant.

In my days of childhood innocence, Grassy Ridge seemed so far away, so inaccessible, so intimidating even to this young ridge runner. Staring with wonder, I tried to picture what was up *there,* way up yonder. I knew Grassy Ridge was quite different from the kinder, gentler, more accessible Big Yellow Mountain, but I still wanted to know what was up *there.*

I was fourteen before I was personally introduced to Grassy Ridge. Just like the Roan, there are a lot of balsam trees, witch hazel shrubs, and a sea of mountain oat grass. What I found most impressive about Grassy Ridge was how high *I* was up there! Nearly seven hundred feet higher than Big Yellow Mountain and Big Hump Mountain, Grassy Ridge looks down on them. I like to think of it as *watching over them.* Perspective.

Up there, way up yonder, I had gained a new perspective on the dips, twists, and turns of the valley below.

Getting from down *here* to *up there,* whether Grassy Ridge, Big, Yellow, Big Hump, or otherwise, is really pretty simple. You just put one foot in front of the other, and keep repeating that until you arrive. That's what I learned to do when I was about six or seven. The front of our house faced almost due East, looking up directly at the dome-shaped outline of Big Yellow Mountain. I have this vague memory of one of our family cookouts, when my parents, and I don't remember who else, gathered up our fixings and headed out on foot to the Big Yellow. I don't think we went all the way to the summit, but we did make it to the southwestern edge.

In the years that followed, most of my Big Yellow pilgrimages, which were often, were done either via motorcycle or 4X4 vehicles. In the mid-seventies, Big Yellow became the property of a conservancy organization, which, in my opinion, was a good thing. Motorized vehicles were banned, and the erosion that had been created by years of vehicular travel slowly began to heal.

Looking like a huge, North-pointing ramp, Big Hump can be seen as far away as Sullivan County, in upper east Tennessee. Driving South on I-26 out of Sullivan or Washington County, I always look for her unmistakable profile. Although Big Hump is just a tad over 100 feet taller than Big Yellow, a West to East/Southeast view of Big Yellow is not possible from that location, the latter being hidden by the sprawling, taller Roan complex.

Neither Grassy Ridge nor Big Hump was my first love. That title is reserved for Big Yellow Mountain, known to most of the locals simply as "the Bald." The Roan Highlands are a curious chain of natural "balds." Among the several "balds," to my mind, Big Yellow wins the beauty contest hands down, although Big Hump and Grassy Ridge are certainly tied as a gorgeous Miss Runner-Up.

Making the three to four-mile trek to Big Yellow from the Roaring Creek Valley would be considered by experienced hikers to be only moderately or even mildly strenuous. The payoff, however, is anything but moderate or mild. To me, it's a religious experience, a bath for the soul, and vitamins for the spirit. I've been to Big Yellow during every season, and try to make it up there no less than once a year, sometimes two or three times.

Let's start with the South-facing side of Big Yellow. You know you've arrived when the trees begin to thin and the mountain oat grass becomes prominent and abundant. Big Yellow's name is attributed to the yellowish hue of that grass. One of the oddities about the Roan Highlands' balds is that they're not naturally high enough in elevation to be above the tree line. For example, Mount Mitchell, highest peak east of the Mississippi, over a thousand feet taller than Big Yellow, is tree-covered with evergreens. Yet, on the higher areas of Unaka, Round Bald, Jane Bald, Grassy Ridge, Big Yellow, Little Hump, and Big Hump, there are no trees. There are a few scrubby little shrubs, but no trees, evergreen or otherwise. On the taller Roan High Knob, however, balsam firs are abundant.

Speaking of trees, on the South-facing side of Big Yellow, you'll see some of the most incredible white oak trees imaginable. They look like they know things, secret things that are centuries-old. I don't have any idea how many centuries these old guardians have stood. They are twisted, gnarled, and battered by lightning, wind, and every weapon in weather's arsenal. Still, they stand.

I feel sure that the oaks on the Bald, perhaps when merely seedlings or saplings, once heard the rumble of the tired feet of the Overmountain Men. Surely, native American children climbed and played on their then-young boughs and branches. No doubt hundreds, and probably thousands of campers, hikers, hunters, and lovers have all alike found shelter and solace in the shadow of these ancient oaks, using some of their dead and lightning-shredded limbs as fuel.

Of the hundreds of times that I have made the pilgrimage to the welcoming summit of Big Yellow, one stands out above all others. It was sometime during winter in the late 1970's. On the Big Yellow, the rime ice had enshrouded every limb, every twig, and every visible sprig of vegetation. With the sky just beginning to turn a pinkish and coral hue in the West, day had begun to fade; night was patiently waiting to cast its peaceful spell over the ridges and hollers. I was there. As many times before, I felt an irresistible urge to be *there*.

My vocabulary is far too poor and inadequate to describe the other-worldly landscape that lay before me. The rime ice was indescribably glorious. I'm sincerely sorry, but *indescribably glorious* is the best that I can come up with. It gleamed like a whole field of pink diamonds in the day's fading light. There was a goodly amount of crusty, wind-tossed snow on the ground, which of course reflected the light to an even greater degree than normal. It was rapturous, and these many decades later, still moves me deeply even to recall it.

A senior lady, in the first church that I served as pastor, told me of her own rime ice experience on the Roan. She said, "Preacher, it was so beautiful I cried." I resonate and concur wholeheartedly with that kindred soul. Some things are just simply that beautiful.

Ancient Celtic Christianity has spoken of *thin places*. These are regarded as special, particular places in which the Divine is experienced more acutely than in ordinary places. Big Yellow is one of my personal *thin places*. It almost seems as if the invisible membrane, separating our dimension from the realm of the great Beyond, is thinner. Those places allow the light from beyond our dimension to be seen more brightly, and its sounds to be heard more clearly. Way up yonder, on the mystic heights, in the deafening silence, and in the golden solitude, fragile life just feels much more sacred.

Chapter 17: The Face of The Deep

...and darkness was upon the face of the deep (Genesis 1:2)

Swaddled in mystery, and written in a poetic cadence, the opening verses of Genesis 1 express the ancient, Jewish account of creation. The latter part of Genesis 1:2 harbors, what is to me a least, a terrifying expression: *"...and darkness was upon the face of the deep."* Darkness, face, deep—these are not merely simple, innocuous expressions. They depict coldness, emptiness, an inky, bottomless void, and most disconcerting of all, *chaos*.

Generally, when we think in terms of the opposite of *somethingness*, we naturally think of *nothingness*. Or perhaps we think of existence and nonexistence. That's completely understandable, unless we are talking about how some of the ancients saw these matters. To the minds of some of those who lived in the hoary mists of antiquity, the opposite of created *somethingness* was not some passive *nothingness,* but something far more malevolent—an active, aggressive, threatening *chaos*. Rather than *something* and *nothing,* some of the ancients conceived of cosmos (order) and chaos (disorder).

Since cosmos and chaos cannot exist simultaneously, one of them has to go. Sometimes cosmos emerges victorious, sometimes not. The capital city in Milton's incomparable epic poem, *Paradise Lost,* for example, was called Pandemonium—chaos reigned supremely, with fallen Lucifer at the helm of hell's government.

Notwithstanding, in the various creation myths, cosmos is the undisputed monarch, otherwise, there's no creation tale to be told. This is where numerous world cultures, including Babylonian, Canaanite, Indian, Israelite, Nordic, and others, incorporate into their creation stories what is known as the

Combat Myth. The very short version of that myth is this: chaotic conditions (usually involving dragons and deep, treacherous waters) had to be violently subdued before cosmos prevailed. Out of a dark, deluged, dragon-haunted chaos, a symmetrical and beautiful cosmos emerged.

Then there's that spine-tingling expression, *the face of the deep.* Let's start with *the deep.* I've always thought that even the sound of the Hebrew word, *tehōm,* translated as "the deep," has an ominous ring to it. It's an incredibly vague yet foreboding description of a vast, cold, pitch-dark, seemingly bottomless expanse of water. In the Hebrew account of creation, God used pre-existing materials to bring cosmos out of the dark abyss of chaos.

Finally, working our way backwards, there's the expression, "the face." We commonly use *face* to describe various entities: the face value of something, the face of the earth, the face of a watch, etc. In this primeval account of creation, *the deep* has a face. Rather than *face,* other descriptions could easily have been chosen: *the surface of the deep, the expanse of the deep, the region of the deep.* No, the deep has a *face.* To me, that makes it much more personal, more threatening, more foreboding.

In its embryonic stage, the created order of the Genesis account was no idyllic, peaceful, melodic event. It began with a formless void, and a dark, threatening *deep* of watery chaos. In something akin to violent conflict, formlessness had to give way to form; void had to be replaced with meaning; darkness was forced to flee from light.

On the unseasonably warm Sunday morning of November 6, 1977, I awoke to the roar of an angry, muddy, raging Roaring Creek. Most of the time when the creek became that full and boisterous, it would become so on the heels of a heavy summer rainstorm. Leading up to that morning, the ground was sloppy-wet with heavy rain, all the smaller streams were full, and the result was inevitable.

That particular Sunday morning, as I often did, weather permitting, I decided to walk the 7/10 mile to church. In front of the church, where Martin's Branch flows beside the far side of the church parking lot, the road was essentially gone. A huge gully had been cut on the near side of the road beside the church, and slabs of asphalt were dislodged in disheveled heaps of disorder. Full, muddy streams were not uncommon in our rainy part of the country, but this was not just a full stream after a deluge of rain, it was a bona fide flood.

It was obvious that there would be no church service that Sunday. Walking back home, I told my parents what had happened. Daddy and I took out on foot to survey the damage. We ended up walking all the way to Plumtree, some six miles away. Someone gave us a lift back. Bridges, foot logs, culverts, and even one resident's hog had been swept away. Driveways, yards, and sections of road were buried in a watery grave.

On that very same date, in the wee hours of the morning, an earthen dam had burst. The unstoppable force of that dam's violent waters took the lives of 39 people on the campus of Toccoa Falls College, in northeast Georgia, some 185 miles away. I'd never heard of Toccoa Falls College before that day. Less than twelve years later, I would be enrolled as an adult student in that very same institution. That connection still intrigues me. I'm not sure what, if anything, to make of it.

The *Great Flood* in my lifetime occurred January 7 and 8, 1998. The November '77 flood paled in comparison. A deep, heavy snow had blanketed the ground in early January. The temperature warmed, the snow began to melt, and then the rains came. All the right elements converged for a perfectly awful storm.

The only damage suffered by Roaring Creek, from the *Great Flood of '98,* was loss of property. Neighboring Carter County, Tennessee suffered the ultimate loss—seven souls perished in the angry waters.

A couple of days after that flood, my wife, daughter, and I drove up from Tennessee to get to my parents' house. I was not remotely prepared for the scene that lay before us.

One of the strangest feelings I ever experienced was attempting to turn up Roaring Creek Road that evening, and being halted by National Guard personnel. Never had I been told that I couldn't drive up Roaring Creek Road. In addition to the troops, there was a mobile Red Cross unit parked at McCoury's Rock Freewill Baptist Church. It was a surreal scene, reminiscent of something you'd see in a disaster movie.

After the vigilant guardsmen patiently explained to us that there was no road on which to travel, they transported us by Humvee to where the bridge at Luther Webb's *used to be.* We had to walk across a makeshift bridge from that point, making the last few tenths of a mile on foot.

Odd as it may sound to attribute human qualities to forces of nature, I've never returned to the same level of trust and consolation toward Roaring Creek since that flood. It was personal—the deep had, once again, assumed a face. That creek used to lull me sleep at night, let me hop and skip across its boulders, and provided refreshment and endless fun in the heat of summer. With trust now washed away, I came to terms with the unsettling realization that this once-friendly, welcoming presence had a sinister side. I was reminded that in the initial stages of creation, it was *darkness*, not light, that was upon the face of the deep. Chaos had temporarily escaped the firm, watchful parameters of cosmos.

Before the flood of '98, a huge, pyramid-shaped boulder stood at the south end of the Big Hole (i.e., a hole/pool of water), which is located diagonally behind my home place. That boulder had stood there my entire life. My familiar friend was gone. Gone where? Who knows, it was simply gone. Just above the Big Hole, the creek used to fork, creating a small, pretty island in between, but not now. One side of the fork had been completely shut down by the rerouted stream.

Another, almost bus-sized boulder, another favorite of mine, was swept away only Lord knows where. I assume that some of those big rocks broke apart under the enormous strain, collision with other jostling boulders, and the hydraulic pressure of the unstoppable force of the raging water. Broken apart or no, in the determined path of that water, they became nothing more than a toddler's bobbing toys. They were found no more.

I've never been one to put much stock in dreams. I'm not of the opinion that every dream holds an important meaning. I remember hearing a counselor say that some dreams are simply your brain's way of taking out the day's garbage. That made sense. But what of recurring dreams? Not the *same dream* per se, but the same *theme*?

For the last several years, probably the last five or six, I've had a recurring dream theme. Almost every night, I dream of water. Sometimes it's an ocean, sometimes it's a river, sometimes it's a lake. Occasionally, my water dream consists of nothing more than a rain shower, a broken water pipe, or a leaking faucet. Not exactly life-threatening, but still, there's water. Much of the time in these water dreams, I'll be fishing. I don't really even enjoy fishing all that much anymore, but in these dreams, I'll sometimes catch a big trout or some other fish. One night, I dreamed that I landed an alligator. I wisely decided to cut the line.

Most of time in these water dreams, I'm neither happy, nor sad, nor frightened. I'm just there, and have no idea why. Most nights when a water dream occurs, which is almost every night, I don't even recognize where I am. Occasionally I will, but most nights not. Sometimes the dreams take on a sinister nature, as reflected in *the face of the deep*. Those types usually involve dark, cold, swiftly flowing rivers, in which I cannot see the bottom. They are quite scary, and very unsettling. In those dreams, I feel a definite existential threat.

I do know that these water dreams have nothing to do with needing to make a trip to the bathroom. My very insightful wife has tried to help me unravel them, but to no avail. I think that if I ever do solve the riddle of the water dreams, somehow, there will be a Roaring Creek connection.

One of my most vivid water dreams occurred sometime not very long after daddy had passed on in 2005. I don't recall the exact date of the dream. I do know that my mother was still living at the time. It could have been a few months or even a few years after daddy passed. It was one of only a handful of dreams that I've ever had that I believe actually meant something. I dreamed that I was in some sort of small, warm ocean. I knew exactly where it was—it was in the meadow directly above my home place, on the opposite side of the road. The light was dim, the sky was steel gray, and a warm, steady drizzle was falling. The trees were barren as in winter, but the air wasn't cold.

My dream was a pluviophile's paradise. A pluviophile is literally defined as a lover of rain; one who finds peace and comfort during rainy days. Friends and family think I'm nuts, but I love dreary, gray, rainy days. Beware! There are more of us out there than you think! To me, there is something comforting about being shrouded in an immense blanket of gray. Weatherwise, my absolute worst days are those in which the sky is clear or mostly clear, it's cold, and the wind is blowing. It depresses me just penning those lines. There's no blanket of protection from the merciless glare of frigid, indifferent space.

This ocean in which I found myself in my dream, felt as if a confluence of warm and cool currents—mostly warm—was gently swirling around me. In the waking world, I float in deep water exactly like a cinder block. Except for a brief, enjoyable afternoon in the Dead Sea a few years ago, I've never been able to float, but in this dream, I was floating. It was as if I were being carried along, ever so tenderly, in some vast amniotic sea of time. Bobbing up and down, slightly left slightly right, up and down, back and forth, I was utterly helpless against the undertow of this gentle ocean's irresistible current. I wasn't afraid. I was powerless, but comfortable, and unafraid.

As the dream sloshed toward a conclusion, looking slightly to my left, I found myself staring at my homeplace and the surrounding property—white vinyl siding; black trim; gray-shingled roof; concrete sidewalk; steep yard; long driveway; creek directly behind the house; the sagging barn that still existed; and the apple trees and yellow locust trees near the barn. In this fleeting moment of observation and contemplation, a sharp dagger of realization suddenly and abruptly pierced my heart: there was no one home. It was my home, but I was disconnected from it, just staring at it from a short distance, while floating and bobbing in a small, warm ocean.

Mommy and daddy made that little piece of earthly heaven, on the banks of Roaring Creek, their home for over half a century. In that dream, they were both forever gone from this life. Like a massive, gray, leaden wave of

sorrow, I knew at that moment in that dream that no one was home, and no one would ever truly be home again.

For a few brief years after my mother's passing, I was determined to rewind, or at least slow down the hands of time, thus continuing the legacy of home. For me, it just didn't work out. Nevertheless, *Place* transcends us all, and will endure till time shall be no more.

Odd as it may seem to have written a book about *Place*, I've slowly come to grips with the fact that *Place*, apart from the people who called it and made it home, is little more than a shell, a pail without water, a body without a soul. In a very different context in which it was originally penned, I have personally found the maxim, *you can't go home again*, to be spot-on. A few can, and I honestly and sincerely applaud them, but I've had to accept the fact that I can't.

More than a dozen Autumns, Winters, Springs, and Summers have passed since that mid-November Saturday, referenced at the outset of this book. As time always does, with indifference and absence of malice, those seasons have borne both weal and woe, joy and sorrow, blue skies and gray.

I cannot help but recall the world-acclaimed Ecclesiastes 3, in which the worldly-wise, life-weary, philosopher-preacher said it this way: "There is a time for everything, and a season for every activity under the heavens...." After the most well-known stanza in his immortal piece, in which the recurring line, "...there is a time for X and a time for Y...," occurs in fourteen pairs, the skeptical old sage then says something that I think is equally if not more gripping. He says, "I have seen the burden God has laid on the human race. He has made everything beautiful in its time. He has also set eternity in the human heart..." (Ecclesiastes 3:10-11, NIV).

We're surely made for something greater than time as we know it. We live between the faint echoes of our Edenic past, while listening for the approaching footsteps of the Age to come. As is always the *ultimate* case, darkness will not cover the face of the deep forever. Chaos will be forced into surrender. Cosmos will eternally prevail.